Elisha Davidson
and the Ispaklaria

Part Two of a Trilogy

by
M.R. ATTAR

HONG KONG · JERUSALEM · USA

Elisha Davidson & the Ispaklaria

Published by MENORAH BOOKS LIMITED

Copyright © July 2015, M. Rhonda Attar

EDITING: Chaim Natan Firszt, Esther Cameron, Ashirah Yosefah
COVER DESIGN: Gal Narunsky
TYPOGRAPHY & LAYOUT: Gal Narunsky
Printed in Jerusalem

All rights reserved. No part of this book may be used or reproduced or
transmitted in any form or by any means, electronic or mechanical, including
photocopying, recording, or by any information storage and retrieval system,
without written permission from the publisher or the author.

INFORMATION AND INQUIRIES: administrator@menorah-books.com

ISBN: 978-1-940516-30-1

FOR ORDERS:
INTERNET: www.menorah-books.com
EMAIL: orders@menorah-books.com

To my mother, Z"L, who made a new day
something wonderful to look forward to.
To my father, Z"L, who made me acutely aware that each day
might behold a separate and mysterious reality.
To my husband Meir, who taught me how to make a day
truly meaningful.
To my daughters Arielle, Moriah and Sivan,
and our boys Motar, Roni and Lior who fill my day
with living, giving and receiving.
And above all, to the Master of the Universe,
in Whose infinite compassion I receive a new day.

CHARACTER MAP

The Davidson Family:

Elisha Davidson a.k.a *The 'Yessod'*: Elisha is almost 11 years old. He lives with his parents in Jerusalem's Old City and just finished sixth grade at North Temple Mount Academy. Elisha loves playing soccer and is addicted to a computer game called 'Flightpilot'. Elisha's birthday is on the 9th of Av.

In Part One of the Elisha Davidson Trilogy, Elisha was anxious to attend the academy's Chamber Summer School Program for the first time, but the program was cancelled due to an unfortunate accident with his teacher, the legendary Professor Bezalel. Shortly afterwards, Elisha discovers an enormous shiny stone embedded into a wall of his home during renovations. After moving the stone into his bedroom, blinding letters of fire burst out of the stone with strange messages. With the help of Rav Kadosh (a great Kabbalah master) who always calls Elisha *The Yessod*, Elisha learns that his mysterious 'mirror stone' is a powerful 'Ispaklaria' – an ancient otherworldly 'ultimate reality', but Elisha doesn't have a clue what any of it means. Elisha only knows that so far, he's discovered a *Choshen* stone (see Glossary), a strange Ispaklaria 'key' with undecipherable symbols, a 'Priest of Light' named Aaron Kohen, and that finding the Ispaklaria has plunged him into the biggest adventure of his life, especially when he finally learns how to actually use it . . . in Part Two of the Elisha Davidson Trilogy, *Elisha Davidson and the Ispaklaria*.

Tamar Davidson: Elisha's mother, Tamar, is a highly-committed Special Education teacher who works with autistic children at the Rita Goldman School in Jerusalem's Old City. Her parents died at a young age and she was raised by her grandfather, 'the illustrious Gabriel Solomon'.

Jessie Davidson: Elisha's father, Jessie, is the Chief Librarian of the Hebrew Literature Archives Institute located in Jerusalem's Old City. He is a leading expert in ancient and rare manuscripts and books. He also has another profession, but that's classified.

Shira Davidson: Elisha's one-year-old sister.

Saba Gabriel: Elisha's great-grandfather (on his mother's side). Saba Gabriel was a famous *Mekubal* (Kabbalah master) and was revered as 'the illustrious Gabriel Solomon'. At 85, due to declining health, he moved in with his granddaughter (Tamar Davidson) and family. He passed away at age 90 in Part One of the Elisha Davidson Trilogy , after telling Elisha that he should move the mysterious mirror stone into Elisha's own bedroom.

Other Characters:

Aaron Kohen a.k.a. *The 'Kohen' (Priest) of Light*: Aaron is a 43-year-old professional mover whose wife passed away six years before he lost both of his teenaged sons in a suicide bus bombing in Jerusalem. Aaron was proclaimed the hero of the tragedy, having hurled the suicide bomber to the back of the bus, which greatly minimized casualties. Aaron mysteriously survived in an inexplicable disaster miracle. Shortly afterwards he was committed to the Jerusalem Psychiatric Hospital, where he was diagnosed with 'Jerusalem Syndrome.' After being released, he became a homeless beggar at the Kotel (the Western Wall) for nearly five years. In Part One of the Elisha Davidson Trilogy, Elisha met Aaron after receiving a fiery message from the Ispaklaria telling him to search for The *Kohen* (Priest) of Light, which turned out to be Aaron. Elisha's parents invited Aaron to live in their home until he got back on his feet, and Elisha's father gave him a job moving boxes in the library's archives. Aaron is a direct descendant of Moses' brother Aaron. He is also one of the '36' (see Glossary), although he is not aware of it.

Akiva Ra'am: Akiva is a 22-year-old Chamber Seven graduate (the highest level attainable in the Chambers Program). He is a fighter pilot in the Israeli Air Force and is engaged to Devorah Barak.

Devorah Barak: Devorah is a 20-year-old Chamber Seven graduate (the highest level attainable in the Chambers Program), originally from Ethiopia. She has the highest IQ ever to attend North Temple Mount Academy and is also a European Champion in Taekwondo. Devorah is engaged to Akiva Ra'am.

Dr. Brody: Psychiatrist and hypnotherapist. Dr. Brody's practice is located in the heart of Tel Aviv. Jonathan Marks is his patient, and through hypnosis sessions he has helped Jonathan regain some of his missing Chambers memories.

Gila: Gila is Shira Davidson's babysitter. She's 15 years old and lives right near the Davidson family.

Girl in the dark, circular, windowless room with the low ceiling: A mysterious girl with otherworldly powers and wisdom. (Her true identity is revealed in Part Three of the Elisha Davidson trilogy.)

Jonathan Marks a.k.a. *The Other*: Jonathan is a 22 year-old journalist living in Tel Aviv. He was top in his class and School President at North Temple Mount Academy and was also the first student to reach Chamber Seven (the highest level in the Chambers Program). Jonathan lost all memory of attending the Chambers Program and left the school and Jerusalem extremely disgruntled. Four years later he started having flashbacks and through hypnotherapy started to remember what transpired in the Chambers. Jonathan is convinced that Professor Bezalel and Principal Oholiov deliberately erased his memory. At North Temple Mount Academy, Jonathan is known as 'The Other' (*Acher*), named after a Talmudic luminary that turned into a heretic.

Josh Kohen: Josh is Elisha's best friend, classmate and neighbor. He is the nephew of Aaron Kohen.

Mrs. Epstein/Great-Aunt Esther: Mrs. Epstein is a Holocaust survivor. She is the great-aunt of Principal Ezra Oholiov and Rebecca Bezalel. She is also a substitute teacher at North Temple Mount Academy. It seems that whenever Great-Aunt Esther is on the scene, the legendary *Avarshina* (phoenix) is not too far away either.

Principal Ezra Oholiov: Ezra is the 42-year-old Principal of North Temple Mount Academy (grades 1–12) and its Chambers Summer School Program (post grades 6–12), both located in Jerusalem's Old City. Ezra is an effective administrator and loyal friend and colleague of Professor Daniel Bezalel, who is also his brother-in-law. Ezra never made it past Chamber One.

Professor Daniel Bezalel a.k.a *The Arranger of Letters*: Professor Bezalel is a 'living legend' at North Temple Mount Academy where he teaches. He is also the genius mastermind behind the school's Chambers Summer School Program and is one of the greatest Fifth Dimensional Luminaries (see Glossary). The 38-year-old scholar is an ordained rabbi and *Mekubal* (Kabbalah master) and Director of the Temple Antiquities Museum in

Jerusalem. He also holds eight PhDs and a professorship in theoretical physics at the University of Cambridge, and was knighted by the Queen of England. Born in England as Paul Montgomery the Third, he converted to Judaism in his teens and then moved to Jerusalem. He is married to Rebecca Oholiov, Principal Ezra Oholiov's younger sister and is a father of four.

In Part One of the Elisha Davidson Trilogy, Professor Bezalel collapses in the middle of teaching his sixth grade class after staring strangely at Elisha. He is left hospitalized and suffering from amnesia and the Chambers Summer School Program is cancelled.

Rav Yehuda Kadosh a.k.a *The Guardian of the Wall*: Rav Kadosh never leaves the Kotel (Western Wall). He is a 70-year-old *Mekubal* (Kabbalah master) and follows the 'traditional' school. Elisha thinks he looks exactly like 'Doc' from Snow White and the Seven Dwarfs. Rav Kadosh is trying his best to help Elisha (despite his shock that Elisha - *The Yessod* turned out to be a child and that Elisha doesn't have even the minutest knowledge of the ancient mystical pathways), but for some reason, he cannot be in the same room with Elisha without aging rapidly. Rav Kadosh is one of the '36' (see Glossary).

Rebecca Bezalel: Rebecca is Professor Daniel Bezalel's wife and Principal Ezra Oholiov's younger sister. She is 36 years old and a mother of four, and she gave birth to their youngest daughter, Alicia, in Part One of the Elisha Davidson trilogy.

PROLOGUE

In the year 2917, there was a servant who had been granted unlimited human wisdom. That was infinitesimal in comparison to Infinite Wisdom. It did, however, make this servant infinitely wiser than any human being who ever was, is, or will be.

At a young age, this servant achieved what no other human being had ever achieved in their lifetime—disillusionment with the entire universe. And that made this servant a master of all the world's illusions.

In the last week of Tammuz, this unique servant faced north and compromised the most resilient illusion of all—the spiral of time. The servant then faced west towards the Ispaklaria and contemplated all the key players in the master plan, feeling absolutely no remorse at leaving them a single week to prove themselves.

Now there was only one thing that the servant could observe through the Ispaklaria. It was chaos. Utter chaos, and it was everywhere.

CHAPTER ONE

Tohu v'bohu — Chaos and Void

A TIME TO WRECK

One minute you think everything's going so great and then . . . *Boom.*

THREE WEEKS. That's what Dr. Allon had just said. "*THREE WEEKS.*" Principal Ezra Oholiov sipped some tea from his melting plastic cup and started calculating. Three weeks had 21 days. 21 days equaled 504 hours, and that's how much time the medical profession was giving his brother-in-law to live. Ezra looked down at the hospital bed and sighed. What happened to Daniel being the recipient of 'the finest medical treatment available'? Well, one look made it pretty obvious. Daniel had had 23 days of full-time hospital care, and he seemed worse every day. Actually, he already looked like a corpse.

Ezra turned away and stared at the Jerusalem skyline out the window. That was life. One minute it was a bright sunny day and Daniel was just routinely teaching his sixth grade class, and then *boom.* One minute he had been *Professor* Daniel Bezalel, the most gifted physics mind in the world, the brilliant mastermind behind North Temple Mount Academy's Chambers program, the *most* important luminary to have walked the planet in thousands of years, and then *boom!* Ezra dumped his tea into the sink. It was too ironic. Daniel couldn't remember a thing! The very pioneer of the Fifth Dimension who unlocked the ancient powerhouses of the human mind couldn't even remember an itsy-bitsy tiny little thing about his extraordinary life.

The hardest part for Ezra was that their 20-year friendship had also been obliterated by that black hole. Not to mention 15 years of marriage with Rebecca, Ezra's younger sister. And it felt utterly surreal to be nothing more than a brand new acquaintance. Rebecca had run out of the room with her hand to her mouth the minute she heard the 'three weeks.' Ezra knew she was trying to spare her husband the anguish of watching her break down in front of him. *Why bother? Daniel was about as attached to her as the doorpost . . .*

Ezra swallowed hard. He also wasn't interested in hearing about Dr. Allon's 'breakthrough-extreme-risk-never-tried-before' complicated surgery that had a 26% chance of success. The only thing Ezra cared about was having them find a cure for Daniel's amnesia. The *one top* item on Ezra's 'to-do list' was to find a trigger, *any* trigger that would bring Daniel's memory back. And yes, he had turned into an obsessed man trying to find one.

He shook his head in frustration while pumping pink hospital antiseptic onto his hands. These doctors were so narrow-minded. Daniel didn't need surgery, he needed *his memory.* If he had his memory, he would know exactly how to cure *himself.* THREE WEEKS. That was the biggest *boom.* Now Ezra was on a deadline. Except that the doctor was wrong. Daniel didn't have 21 days. Ezra was 100% positive that if a death verdict came in,

TOHU V'BOHU — CHAOS AND VOID 3

then it would surely be 15 days. That was it. 15 days if Daniel didn't regain his memory.

Ezra pulled the curtain closed around the hospital bed just as Daniel's eyes flickered open.

Daniel searched the room and called out, "Ezra?"

"I'm right here."

"I forgot . . . a young man was here with a message for you. Look in the drawer . . ." Daniel motioned with his head to the hospital cart near his bed.

Ezra pulled opened the small aluminum drawer and found an envelope. It was addressed to 'Principal Ezra Oholiov' and written in flawless penmanship that Ezra instantly recognized. He knew he should throw it right into the garbage. Instead, he unfolded the small note and read the immaculate handwriting.

Restore my memory and I'll restore Professor Bezalel's Jonathan Marks, a.k.a. The Other ☺

Ezra closed his eyes and crunched the paper in his fist . . . *Be careful what you wish for* . . . He should have added one important caveat—*any* trigger *except* for Jonathan Marks. No one needed to press 'start' on the 'End of Days'.

Daniel's hoarse and labored voice suddenly broke his chain of thoughts.

"Don't do it. Whatever is troubling you, don't do it."

Ezra looked hopefully and expectantly at his brother-in-law, maybe some part of him was coming back, but his hopes were shattered with the next sentence.

"I wish I did know you. I'm sorry that I don't, but I'd be blind not to know that whoever you are, you would do anything for me."

Ezra's eyes were downcast, but Daniel continued.

"That young man was troubled. Don't do anything he asks."

Ezra breathed out a long sigh of relief. Even if Daniel didn't know the first thing he was talking about, he couldn't help holding on to that old comfort zone where all he had to do was to faithfully follow Daniel's instructions.

Jonathan Marks slammed hard on the brakes and then jolted back and forth in his seat. It was a delayed reaction and too late. He angrily smacked his palm against the steering wheel. A goat. What in the world was a *goat* doing wandering in the street just two blocks from his apartment? If he was driving on one of Israel's peripheral roads, OK, he might even expect a herd crossing, but *not* in the center of Tel Aviv! And yup, he had hit it. He had seen it go down, beige scruffy beard and all, and had felt the impact. He had even heard a loud bleaty groan.

The last thing Jonathan was in the mood for was carnage and car repairs. It was his own fault too. He had been practicing Chamber Five permutations in his head while driving, which was probably ten times worse than composing a long SMS, even though his eyes never left the road. He flung open his car door, thoroughly disgusted, and went to the front of his car to inspect the damage. When he looked down at the fender, he couldn't help wincing. The goat's body was totally mutilated from the impact.

"Hey, are you OK?"

Jonathan looked up. It was nosey neighbor #2 walking his pug dog.

"I'm fine," Jonathan called back.

"That empty bicycle box has been here since last night. I told Newman's kids that if they didn't throw it into the garbage bin, I'd report them to the municipal sanitation department. But those kids are hooligans."

Jonathan looked under the front wheels again. He *was* looking at a goat—or at least what was left of one. Wasn't he? Jonathan suddenly froze and a jolt of terror adrenaline surged through his body. He was barely able to ask, "Would you validate—I'm sorry, would you repeat what you just said?"

"The Newman kids are hooligans," his neighbor said while tying his dog's leash to a fence. Then he walked over and gave the dead goat a hard kick. The movement shocked Jonathan, and it split the goat's body in two.

"Hey, *stop!*"

"Oh, sorry. Did you want to leave the box under the car and take pictures of it or something? Actually that's a good idea. You could sue them, but you know, on the other hand, it's not like there's any real damage."

Jonathan instinctively shut his eyes tightly as he felt his whole body diving into a high-speed free fall. He braced himself on the hood of his car and then felt his knees absorbing the shock. When he landed, he slowly opened his eyes and stared underneath the car. There it was. A large dilapidated cardboard box crunched under the front wheels. No goat. Not even a single goat hair.

"I *told* those kids to move it. I told them someone could have an accident."

Right, and you couldn't put the fatal road hazard in there yourself, Jonathan thought as he tugged away at the box with his hands shaking uncontrollably. He *knew* exactly what was happening to his mind right now, and he was doing his best not to have an all-out panic attack.

The minute Jonathan entered his apartment, he flopped onto the sofa like a condemned man. He shouldn't have been cramming through all the Chambers, especially *not* Chamber Five, and now he had gotten his death sentence. Jonathan stared at the ceiling. Maybe it wasn't the cramming. Maybe his contact with Professor Bezalel, or what was left of him, had triggered it. *Maybe* it was his hypnotherapy sessions with Dr. Brody, trying to regain all seven years' worth of his missing Chamber memories at once, and this was just one more bad side effect of the hypnosis. *Or* maybe it was simply and obviously Chamber Five. Mastering transformation was seriously advanced and dangerous—*don't try it at home, never mind on the road*. Jonathan arched his head back and exhaled slowly. What difference did it make? The bottom line was the same. He was probably in *'tohu v'bohu'*, otherwise known as chaos and void, a debilitating state of mind where initiates got stuck between 'formation' and 'action'. It's when you could perfectly visualize transformations in your mind, but couldn't actually bring them into physical existence. Jonathan had seen first-hand what happened to Chamber Five initiates who got stuck in *'tohu v'bohu,'* and he couldn't even bear to think about it. Instead, he jumped off the sofa while wiping his palms on his pants.

Self-diagnosis first. He surveyed the room carefully and reminded himself that despite his personal doomsday crisis, he needed to be systematic, and most importantly, to start small and simple. He went over to the fridge and pulled out a tomato. He plucked off the leafy stem and placed the stem on the white counter. He drew a circle around it with a black magic marker. It wasn't lost on him that for thousands of years his predecessors would have required 35 continuous hours to achieve what he was about to do in only 35 minutes, thanks to Professor Bezalel's intensive training. He also knew that four years ago he could have done it in 3.5 seconds, and that the Professor himself could have accomplished it in .035 seconds or less.

Jonathan wasn't deterred. He closed his eyes and watched the static in his mind. The usual non-stop kaleidoscope of images flashed by continuously, each image superimposed on the last. He carefully performed preliminary breathing and focusing exercises until he formed the object into a perfectly sharp thought. He was highly aware that automatic speech was his biggest adversary. The *real* essences of objects were words, and the words consisted of letters, mental conceptual letters that were built by his voice, carved by his breath and engraved with his speech. He elevated his image through the four illusive reality barriers until he reached nothingness, and then the tomato stem ceased to exist. Now was the critical part. Jonathan voiced the permutations along with head motions to correspond to the shape of the vowels. He then meticulously directed his speech in six physical directions envisioning two triangles overlaid into a star and brought the influx of his newly-formed image into the physical world. Jonathan smiled. He knew he had executed the transformation permutations to perfection.

A spider with the same dark green color as the tomato stem was now scampering up the kitchen splashboard at full speed. *Next.* Without unsettling his state of mind, Jonathan scanned the kitchen. He noticed that his black belt was hanging off the kitchen chair. He focused on the exact permutations and was satisfied to see a deadly-looking black snake undulating to life. Now he was ready to face his *bigger* problem. He needed 'validation'. He needed to find out if the permutations were actually altering nature or if they were *only in his mind*. His doorbell rang. He flinched slightly. He was surprised to have opportunity number one so soon. The fact of the matter was that he wasn't really sure if he even wanted 'validation'. He suddenly felt nauseous, like he was about to get the results of a fatal blood test. He reminded himself that he needed to be systematic and to just do it! He grabbed the snake off the chair, put it around his neck and then looked through the peephole. Perfect. It was Mrs. Sobol from 4B. She'd freak. He opened the door.

"Hi. I'm here for the House Committee," she said in an official voice.

No reaction.

She tapped her clipboard. "We're voting on switching landscapers."

Jonathan grabbed the snake's head and put it right under his chin. It started to slowly slither through his fingertips and was about to coil around Mrs. Sobol's pen.

"I'm so sorry, did I interrupt you while you were getting dressed? How embarrassing. I can come back later . . ."

Jonathan did his best to hide his utter despair as he ticked off the first box he could find on the page. It *was only* in his mind . . . .

Jonathan closed the door and threw the snake off his neck and watched it slither across the tiled floor. He felt sick to his stomach and then immediately convulsed when a wild-velocity freefall sensation hit him again as he grabbed hold of the door handle. He *was* in *tohu v'bohu*. Jonathan gagged, ran to the bathroom, and then lay down on his bed and closed his eyes. He reviewed his

TOHU V'BOHU — CHAOS AND VOID

two choices. *One: be locked up in an insane asylum for the rest of my life. Two: Go crawling back to Professor Bezalel and Principal Oholiov and actually beg them to perform one of their selective memory erasures.*

Jonathan couldn't accept either choice. He felt all the blood rushing to his head in a violent rage. None of this would be happening if he still had unrestricted access to the Foundation Vault! It was because they had locked him *out* that he was flunking Chamber Five in flying colors. They hadn't just wiped away all his Chambers memories four years ago; they'd *killed* his fifth dimensional self. The snake slithered into the bedroom and Jonathan started stomping on its head with his heel. *There HAD to be a third*—something else, something within his reach—to UNDO IT!

Once the snake was pulverized beyond recognition, a single thought drifted into Jonathan's mind. LOCK DOWN. It was only a small band-aid, but it was all he had. He needed to gain control of his imagination *immediately*. In Chamber Five a vivid imagination was your best asset and also your worst enemy. Jonathan had spent two years being the recess guard for Chamber Five initiates, so he knew exactly how badly things could turn out. His memory flashed back to Simon Zoma who was just quietly practicing his Chamber Five permutations in a corner of the Foundation Vault when he suddenly became convinced that he was in the Halloween Chainsaw Massacre movie. It was gruesome, and Jonathan knew it was going to get much worse, because he'd seen the horror film himself. *Don't go there,* Jonathan quickly reminded himself: He refocused on how he had alerted Professor Bezalel and Principal Oholiov just in time. Just in time for them to selectively delete all of Simon's Chambers memories while Jonathan watched five years of intensive training go down the drain. It might have been compulsory protocol, but Jonathan had nightmares for weeks.

Jonathan exhaled loudly. LOCK DOWN. Imagination *lock down*. That was the key to Chamber Five survival. Most of North Temple Mount Academy's students had made it through Chambers One through Four, but only half the students were allowed to continue on to Chamber Five, and out of those, only about a quarter ever made it to Chamber Six.

It didn't matter how much time Principal Ezra Oholiov had spent screening the kids beforehand. They used to lie through their teeth and right to his face, starting with Question One: Which sci-fi, fantasy, disaster or horror movies have you seen? Question Two: Which sci-fi, fantasy, disaster or horror books have you read? Question Three: Which computer games do you play? That was when those kids everyone used to feel so sorry for because their parents had forbidden TV/computers as contraband, ended up having a major advantage—most of the time, but not always. Jonathan had personally watched, read and played everything out there, and he had *never* contracted *tohu v'bohu*. It must have been because his advanced mind also knew how to LOCK DOWN.

Jonathan's phone buzzed. It was Yoram, his editor. The call was sobering and a great lock-down. It reminded Jonathan that he had a realistic deadline to meet, and it wasn't cramming seven years of Chambers training into two weeks to be ready for the 9th of Av.

He went over to his laptop and started working on his article. Chamber Five was OUT. He was going to lock down and also backtrack. He'd return to Chamber Four and get a firmer foundation, even *without* the Foundation

Vault. Right now, his career advancement was going to be the only thing on his mind. He'd finish the article in a few hours and personally put it on Yoram's desk. Jonathan jerked his foot and looked down. His grotesque phantom snake was *back*.

He grabbed it and pushed the slithery thing through each one of his belt loops. He buckled it by forcing the snake to swallow its own tail. It was a belt.

For the 25,648th morning of his life, Rav Kadosh basked in the shade cast by the Western Wall. Upon raising his eyes to the sky, he observed that it was another perfect summer day. He kissed the Wall goodbye and then walked backward for 30 seconds. Two minutes after turning around, he was inside the cool Jerusalem stone interior of his modest abode. He stood on tiptoe to hang his black hat on the coat rack and then started unbuttoning his black overcoat. He rubbed his hands together and cheerfully announced, "Well my dear wife, the race for the 9th of Av is ON!"

"You've been saying that for years and nothing ever happens," his wife said as she reached for a chess set on top of a tall bookcase.

Rav Kadosh shook a pointed finger in the air. "My dear Bruria! This year is *entirely* different." He then raised his hands dramatically, like an orator, and boomed out, "On this coming 9th of Av, on the most monumental day in the cycle of time, the darkest and brightest day of our human existence, the moment designated from time immemorial for the greatest tragedies or the greatest blessings, on this very year, it's going to be *win all or lose all!*"

"You also say *that* every year and nothing ever happens. Are you going to be black or white?"

"White . . . But I'm telling you that I just found out that *this* week is the critical week! This week will determine who is destined for greatness! I heard it straight from one of my *most* reliable sources. We don't even need to wait for the 9th of Av to arrive! Whoever attains *true* wisdom by the end of the month of Tammuz, will have what it takes to *win-all* in Av!"

"Hmmm . . . was it my mother or my *father,* may they both rest in peace?" Bruria asked as she started arranging her chess pieces on the board and then grumbled, "Nu, set up your pieces."

Rav Kadosh put his king and queen in place and then cleared his throat. "It was your father of blessed memory, but that doesn't have to *mean* that it's the end of the world."

Bruria started humming a high-pitched tune while arranging Rav Kadosh's pieces for him.

Rav Kadosh sat back in his chair and immediately changed the subject. "I know you want to *know* who's in the race this year."

"I already know," she said. "Professor Bezalel's highly trained Fifth Delusional Luminaries. What else is new? Now move."

"They're called Fifth *Dimensional* Luminaries, my dear."

"Believe me, with only two Chamber Seven graduates and Professor Bezalel *kaput,* they're delusional."

"Yes, such a shame. Such a shame! But this year," Rav Kadosh said with excitement as he moved his pawn, "we have fresh new potential—Elisha Davidson and Aaron Kohen!"

Bruria grimaced. "Right. The insane beggar and Ga-

TOHU V'BOHU — CHAOS AND VOID   13

briel Solomon's great grandchild . . ."

"As extraordinary as it may seem, young Elisha Davidson *is* the *Yessod* and Aaron Kohen is not only a direct descendant of Moses's brother Aaron, he's also one of the 36. And when has there *ever* been a Kohen that was one of the 36?!"

Bruria raised an eyebrow and then moved her black pawn. "Big deal. You're also one of the 36, and where's that gotten us? And last time I looked around, no one on this planet would have merited *one* freak of nature, never mind *two*! So that just leaves a couple of miscreations fumbling in the dark. At least the 'delusionals' have wisdom."

Rav Kadosh twiddled his thumbs before deciding on his next move and asked, "Guess who I'm counting on?"

"That's obvious. You're Old School. So it's the fool and the child."

Rav Kadosh nodded his head. That was most certainly true. And if his instincts were right, he was aligning himself with the *ancient* school—never mind 'old.' He pulled at his long white beard.

Bruria interrupted his thoughts: "What is it? There's something *else* you're not telling me."

Rav Kadosh took off his glasses and started cleaning them carefully. Last night had been the seventh night in a row that he had had the same recurring dream—a spectacular vision in which he had merited setting his eyes on the legendary Shamir. Unfortunately, he had never actually seen it clearly, nor could he make out exactly what he was looking at, but he was absolutely certain that it *was* the Shamir. He knew that he could never tell Bruria about it. After all, she might think he was losing his mind. Instead, he leaned over the chess set with a secretive air.

"Well. There's also some very unfortunate news. Your grandnephew twice removed—he's on his way back."

"Wouldn't you know it. I told Fanny years ago that that boy was a bad seed. She was always raving about him, 'Jonathan this and Jonathan that.' He was always too smart and talented for his own good. That boy has a mean competitive streak. Mark my words, he'll catch up fast, and then you're 'lose-all' this year."

Rav Kadosh sighed in agreement. "Which is why I have decided on this single occasion that emergency measures are in order."

Bruria moved her queen and then sat back in her chair. "So, *that's* the something *else* that you weren't telling me about!"

Rav Kadosh nervously tapped his fingers on the chess set and started speaking quickly. "You see, the boy found an Ispaklaria! An *Ispaklaria*! That changes everything!"

Bruria became thoughtful. "An Ispaklaria? Hmmm. Why would *anyone* give *them* an Ispaklaria! That certainly seems unwise . . ." She studied the board and griped under her breath, "Why that's as absurd as expecting a two year old to fly a plane."

"Exactly, my dear! Which is why just this once, and for an extremely limited amount of time, mind you, one time only, I have decided . . . to become personally involved and enlighten them."

Bruria knocked Rav Kadosh's queen off the board with her knight. "Well, now all your sneaking around is clear as the light of day, isn't it? It's that *boy* that has aged you over 20 years in just a few weeks . . . IF that boy *is* the *Yessod*, we both know he's your death sentence!"

"No, *no*, I've been *very* careful. I have severely

TOHU V'BOHU — CHAOS AND VOID

limited my time with him. I *only* trained him when the miscreation Kohen was around to protect me. And I've been extremely efficient to teach them exactly what they need to know, and of course in the shortest amount of time possible."

"So, now they're even *more* clueless," she said as she made another move.

Rav Kadosh looked down at his pieces completely flustered. "Now, now, Bruria, you know that reaching the 9th of Av finish line will be well worth any and all of our small and humble sacrifices."

"You mean *yours*. I've always told you that your overzealousness would catch up with you one day. Don't expect me to be schlepping chicken soup to the hospital if you end up like Professor Bezalel."

"I wouldn't dream of it, my dear."

Bruria looked up from the chess board. "Consider this, *dear* husband. When my father, of blessed memory, was *alive*, he kept a 'do not disturb' sign on his study door 24/7 and was interrupted in life-and-death situations ONLY. So what in the world could possibly compel him to disturb his *eternal* peace NOW?" Bruria lifted her queen and held it tightly in her fingertips. "I'll tell you what! A life-and-death situation of incalculable proportions. Yours! It's YOU who won't make it until the end of this 'critical' week. The *Yessod* will kill you and then it will be lose-all *forever*." She moved her queen triumphantly and announced, "Checkmate."

Bruria then adjusted the cushion she was sitting on and leaned back comfortably in her chair while folding her arms. "Now, my dear husband, I think it's about time that you *really* tell me what it is that you're not telling me about."

Elisha kicked the wall next to his bed. He was having the worst summer of his life. It was bad enough that he had had a front row seat when Professor Bezalel collapsed in their classroom, but it was even worse that they had cancelled the Chambers Summer School Program. *Hello boring summer.* And just when things were looking up and he had found his cool mirror stone in the wreckage of their bathroom renovations, it turned out the thing was ... Elisha glanced at the massive mirror stone that took up a whole wall of his bedroom. Was a ... what *was* it, *really*? Rav Kadosh called it an Ispaklaria, but what was *that*? He also called it twenty other things that made no sense either, like a 'world without its mask' or 'ultimate reality.'

The only thing Elisha knew was that blinding letters of fire with strange messages had blasted out of the stone, and once a massive tornado snake swimming in a bloodbath. Elisha kicked the wall again. It was forever horrible that his great-grandfather had died and left him alone and on his own. Elisha missed him so badly that he even thought he heard him calling his name from the Ispaklaria.

Now Rav Kadosh was the only person around that could help. But Rav Kadosh always seemed desperate to get rid of him, and his explanations only made everything more confusing. Like the stupid piece of paper he was staring at ... the printout from his father's library that had 'decoded' the strange symbols on the Ispaklaria's key. Now instead of symbols there were at least words and numbers that he could read. Elisha didn't blink at the page for 30 straight seconds hoping that he'd get some kind of flash.

TOHU V'BOHU — CHAOS AND VOID

```
Four dimensions of nothingness:
The Illusion of Time
1: 2928 3338
2: 3408 3830
3: 5766 5777
4: EIGHTH KINGDOM
```

He closed and rubbed his eyes. Nothing!

Why didn't Aaron know *anything?* Elisha had been so *sure* when he found him that everything would fall into place. After all, he was supposed to be the *Kohen,* the "Priest of Light." OK, he was nice, but how did he get to be a "Priest of Light" if he was homeless, nearly blown to bits in a terrorist bombing, and kind of a . . . psycho. Even Elisha's parents had felt so sorry for Aaron that they invited him to live in their house until he 'got back on his feet again'.

Elisha could hear the morning sounds of Jerusalem's Old City streets bustling to life through his open window until they were drowned out by loud screaming and crying noises. He blocked them out. It was only his little sister Shira starting off the day with one of her usual tantrums. *What was it this time?* Did the single pacifier they kept in the house get lost *again?* Elisha pulled the sheet over his head and tried for the twentieth time to focus on the piece of paper in his hands. *Shira sounded like she was being murdered.* It was Dad for sure. He must have poured one milliliter less of apple juice into her bottle. Elisha covered his ears and felt his throat catch. Wasn't it bad enough that his parents were fighting about him all the time and he wasn't even sure why? What ever happened to happily ever after? How about even *one* thing working out right? Elisha held up the piece of paper again. He instinctively knew that his whole life depended on understanding those numbers . . . at least the first underlined ones. The Ispaklaria was stuck on them or as Rav Kadosh had said "someone had child-proofed it" to be stuck on them. He threw off the sheet in frustration. What was the use? And why was he even bothering to try? Rav Kadosh had told him that in order to 'receive' something from the Ispaklaria, he had to first become a 'selfless nothing'. Right . . . how was that even possible? It suddenly occurred to him that the best way to do that was to go back to sleep.

Ezra was rushing through the narrow cobblestone alleyways to make it to the school building in time. He kept repeating to himself: *The end is embedded in the beginning, and the beginning in the end.* It was one of Daniel's favorite lines whenever they walked through the Old City together. But how could he apply it to Daniel, when they didn't even know how his end began?

He followed along the Cardo and glanced down at the thousands of years of history below his feet. In this one spot there was a long chain of beginnings and ends. The kings of Israel had built an outer city wall, and the Romans had turned it into a highway. The Byzantines had transformed it into a colonnaded avenue, and the Crusaders had made it into a marketplace. The Ottomans had turned it into a garbage dump, and now, of course, it was none other than an expensive boutique shopping mall. *Vanity of vanities, all is vanity, said Kohelet.* Nothing lasts forever . . . The Old City of Jerusalem was eternal, but not its kings or conquerors, and *not its Fifth Dimensional Luminaries* . . . .

TOHU V'BOHU — CHAOS AND VOID

Ezra quickly turned into a narrow entryway that belied the large school complex cloistered behind it. He then followed a long Jerusalem-stone passageway until it opened into a spacious courtyard graced with seven arched gates. The assembly hall towered to the right with its twelve-sided stained-glass skylight. Ezra turned left and climbed up the steps two at a time. He rushed into his office just as his laptop chimed and a recurring appointment flashed onto his screen: *Chamber Seven Graduate Assembly.* Ezra knew that calling it an 'assembly' was pathetic, and he was seriously wondering if all the effort had been worthwhile. In the course of eleven years 639 students had passed through North Temple Mount Academy's "Chambers Program" under his administration, and only *three* students had ever made it to their Chamber Seven graduation. Out of the three, only two would knock on his door in five minutes. And they were the last hope. Devorah Barak and Akiva Ra'am. They were almost as obsessed with saving Daniel as he was; but Devorah was busy studying for her psychometric exam while training for her upcoming Taekwondo competition, while Akiva was a fighter pilot in the Air Force. Luckily, he was on one of his rare and coveted seven-day leaves. They were also planning their wedding, which was only three months away.

The minute they entered his office, all of Ezra's misgivings dissipated. He would go through ten more sets of 639 students if he could be assured of turning out two more graduates as worthy as these.

Akiva practically glowed with rock-of-Gibraltar stability in his perfectly-pressed uniform. All his body language and each facial feature exuded his true personality—serious, intelligent, capable, and trustworthy.

He also happened to have lightning-fast reflexes. Those basic attributes with Chamber Seven empowerment made a formidable combination. He was also a straight-by-the-books kind of guy, which earned him Ezra's highest admiration, although he knew that Daniel had thought it was Akiva's biggest shortcoming. Nothing had come easily to Akiva, and that's what made him stupendous. He had even been held back a grade when he had transferred to North Temple Mount, but had amazingly caught up. Akiva was living testimony that sheer willpower held the key to personal transformation.

On the other hand, small and lithe Devorah with her face that could "launch a thousand ships" was a lethal walking illusion. Behind that facade was not only the highest IQ that ever passed through North Temple Mount Academy, but a heart courageous enough to lead a thousand ships into battle against insane odds and win. Devorah had proven herself long before graduating the Chambers program: at the tender age of nine she had walked hundreds of miles along a dangerous escape route from Ethiopia to the Sudanese border. A trek that was so treacherous and perilous that it had taken the lives of her pregnant mother and a younger brother.

She walked into the office wearing an all-white dress that contrasted intensely with her dark skin. Devorah actually had a sizable wardrobe of white. No gold jewelry, not ever, just a single silver snake insignia ring that marked her as a descendant of the tribe of Dan. Devorah was practical. As a Chamber Seven graduate she had unlimited access into the Foundation Vault, and there violating the dress code wasn't just a trifling break in protocol; it was suicide.

Ezra immediately searched her face for some semblance of good news. She was coming back from a uni-

TOHU V'BOHU — CHAOS AND VOID

fications session in the Foundation Vault, and Ezra was hoping against hope that she would return with something that could help Daniel. He didn't waste time when they arrived: "Dr. Allon just told me that Professor Bezalel has three weeks max."

Akiva furrowed his brow. "He's going to die on the 9th of Av. Our worst case scenario . . ."

"Right. We've only got 15 days left. We're running out of time."

Devorah looked down at the floor and took a measured breath. "No. He's *not* going to die on the 9th of Av. There's only seven days left."

Ezra jumped up from his desk. "What! How's *that* possible?"

"I can't explain it, I don't know why it's happening, but there's some type of critical acceleration taking place this week."

"No," Ezra protested. "*No.* We're still in the month of *Tammuz.* Things aren't supposed to be hastened until the month of Av."

Devorah replied in a resigned voice. "I just used *ten* different seals. There's a contraction, and we only have until the end of Tammuz."

Ezra glanced at his calendar. "Devorah, this is insane. Is *that* all you came back with!?"

"No . . ." Devorah hesitated. Principal Oholiov was going to completely freak out; she'd have to deliver the news in bit-size pieces. "I wasn't alone in the Foundation Vault."

Ezra almost choked. *How in the world had Jonathan gained access to the Foundation Vault!*

Devorah knew she shouldn't be reading his mind, but then, really, he shouldn't be thinking at full volume! And why in the world was *Jonathan* even on his mind?

He must be so stressed out that he was turning paranoid. She looked directly at him and said. "It's *not* Jonathan. But we do have a *new* Chambers graduate."

Ezra reached for his chair and in the calmest voice he could muster, he slowly asked her, "Please explain . . ."

"I just found a highly trained Fifth Dimensional Luminary. Someone trained by Professor Bezalel himself. And this person is SO good, I think that she might have reached his level."

Ezra looked totally shell-shocked. "*She?* Hold on. Professor Bezalel *never* trained anyone outside of the Chambers Program."

"She somehow *did attend* the Chambers Program. She knew all of our names, our *real* names."

Ezra headed to his safe to retrieve his list of 639 students. Before he got to it, Devorah had unlocked the safe and the door swung open. "Don't do that, OK? My fingerprint works fine," he chided her and then to himself he started grumbling. "Great! We've got another loose cannon to deal with! That's all we need—another *Other*!"

Devorah turned around. "Wait. It gets stranger. She attended *all 11 years* of the program since its revival, which explains why she has such advanced empowerment."

Ezra gripped a large grey file and then held it in place. "*There is NO student that's spent 11 years in the Chambers Program!!*"

"I know, and here's the thing. I don't think she was always *physically* in the classes either."

Ezra felt his head starting to spin. He let go of the file and faced Devorah. " O—K—, so you want to tell me that we've started a Chambers Program 'correspondence school' that I'm not aware of?"

Devorah cringed. "Apparently."

Akiva remained completely silent, taking in every word while trying his best to analyze the situation.

Ezra closed the safe and returned to his desk carrying the file. He knew all too well that it only took two years in the Chambers Programs for their initiates to start gaining minimal empowerment. Unfortunately, Ezra himself, hadn't made it past Chamber One, but that was, of course, because he had started way too late in life. But, *11 years!*

Ezra was flipping through the file. "Alright. So she's probably what, 23 or 24?"

Akiva leaned forward in his chair. "Minimum, or she could be much, much older. Let's put her in a range of anywhere between 23 and up to 90."

Ezra suddenly brightened. "This could actually be good news. If Professor Bezalel was her mentor, she'd obviously want to help him, right?"

Devorah wavered slightly before delivering her last blow. "*Except* that the presence I encountered in the Foundation Vault was waiting for the *very person* who destroyed Professor Bezalel . . . a person that I sensed she would go to any length to protect. She's not *with* us."

Ezra's mind flashed back to Jonathan's note. "Well, this is simply not acceptable. I want to talk to her! You have to find her right away!"

Akiva cleared his throat. "Sure. Let's just tell her to report to the Principal's office a.s.a.p."

Ezra started nervously tapping his pen on this desk. "Come on, Devorah. Just turn on that . . . that internal homing system of yours."

Devorah could still picture the impenetrable three-dimensional space vividly. *The room was roughly circular. It had a low ceiling. The walls were black. Dark black.*

There wasn't any light in the room. She stared straight at Ezra without blinking and said, "She doesn't want to be found."

Ezra buried his head in his hands. "*We have seven days.*"

Akiva stood up. "We still have plenty of time, and I'm heading straight to the Wall."

Ezra nodded at them as they left, but couldn't help thinking that at this point, the 'End of Days' start button was looking more attractive by the minute.

CHAPTER TWO

Kings and Camp Counselors

A TIME TO KEEP

The dream was going great until Elisha heard loud knocking on the goalpost. *Since when did people have to knock to get into a stadium?* He opened his eyes and turned his head toward the door. It was wide open, and Aaron's large and hulking frame was practically filling up the whole doorway. There was a small Red Sox baseball cap lying flat on his head, and two whistles were hanging off his neck.

"Don't you ever go sayin' that the Kohen of Light doesn't do his homework," Aaron said as he waved a torn piece of notebook paper high into the air. "I know what our secret coded numbers mean!"

"Yeah. Right." Elisha grumbled and faced his wall again.

Aaron raised both eyebrows. *Oops, Kiddo woke up on the wrong side of the bed this mornin'.* Aaron had been doing it himself for five years straight. Funny though, just when he had switched sides, it looked like Elisha was going in the other direction. Aaron stretched his arms high over his head. From the minute he had woken

25

up this morning, his gut had been telling him that he'd wasted enough time and now he needed to make up for it. He called out to Elisha: "Hey! Would you lighten up a bit?" Zero reaction. Aaron clapped his hands. "Fine. Go back to sleep. But by the way, your father just happened to ask me this mornin' how all the computer lessons you were givin' me were comin' along. So don't mind me," Aaron said as he sat down at Elisha's desk and cracked his knuckles, "while I take over your computer all day and practice FreeCell."

It worked. Elisha moaned and reluctantly got up. "OK, so why do you think you know?"

The enthusiasm in Aaron's voice instantly returned. "You see, there I was fillin' in all those endless new employee forms today in that basement of your Dad's library."

"The archives," Elisha corrected him.

"Right, the archives, and then I saw it!"

"Saw what?"

"Right on the wall. There were our mysterious numbers. And they were *huge*, for all eyes to see. 1T, 2T, 1M, 2M. But of course, we don't need the M's and then there were B's before it I think."

Elisha had no idea what Aaron was going on about.

"You see down in the archives, they file everythin', but they've got to keep it real organized, right? So the system is different color codes by years in history. And since they want to make sure no one messes up, they've got these massive signs on the wall. And then I saw it. The blue one, 1T, just starin' me in the face. 1T 2928-3338." Aaron smiled smugly, "So, I just read the writin' on the wall!" When Elisha didn't react, Aaron practically shouted. "They're *not* just plain numbers! They're *years*!

KINGS AND CAMP COUNSELORS

Hebrew calendar years! 'The Illusion of Time', *get it*?? Isn't it amazing what just one small dash can do between numbers?" Aaron ceremoniously made a huge dash between the numbers on his torn paper and then snorted with satisfaction.

Elisha quickly pulled the print out from under his pillow. He actually couldn't believe that he hadn't figured it out himself. He looked at the wrinkled writing and imagined dashes between all the numbers and read the page out loud.

Four dimensions of nothingness:
The Illusion of Time
1: 2928-3338
2: 3408-3830
3: 5766-5777
4: EIGHTH KINGDOM

Aaron repeated slowly, "1T 2928–3338. And 1T is the code for—"

"First Temple!" Elisha shouted, as his stomach started uncontrollably doing cartwheels. "Wait. And the second one, 3408–3830. That's the Second Temple period!" Elisha chided himself for being so stupid. Even the lousiest of Professor Bezalel's students had those numbers drilled into their heads. They were the Hebrew calendar years that each of the Temples had stood before being destroyed. They both had lasted about 400 years. How had he ever missed it?

Aaron was nodding and smiling ear to ear. "Yup. 2T. That one was in grey color-code."

"But wait!" Elisha shouted. "What's *5766–5777*? That's like now! 5777 is the Hebrew calendar year *now.*

Did they have that one color-coded too?"

"Nope. That one is a dud . . ."

Elisha started racking his brains, but couldn't think of anything historically significant that had happened 11 years ago that would make it onto a timeline.

"Nothing on the wall that was even close to that weird Eighth Kingdom one you liked either," Aaron added as he pulled off the Red Sox cap from the top of his head and started forcing it onto Elisha's.

"What are you doing?" Elisha asked as he threw the baseball cap onto his desk.

"Hey!" Aaron shouted. "I'm prepping you for your big day and you're . . . wait, hold on a minute, I'll be right back," Aaron said as he dashed out of the room.

The moment he was alone, Elisha felt the shell-shock take effect immediately. It was clear that Aaron was raring to go. They were actually going to use the freaky Ispaklaria mirror stone now, right now, like when Aaron got back, now *now*. Well, they did crack the code. But did that mean there was nothing to be scared about? Elisha reached for the baseball cap and put it firmly on his own head, trying his best to stop seeing outtakes from every horror flick he had ever seen.

Aaron came back with a large knapsack and handed it to Elisha with a wide smile.

"What's this for?" asked Elisha.

"Well, you're not goin' to go into some unknown 'ultimate reality' unprepared, are you?"

"But Rav Kadosh said I actually don't *go* anywhere. He said I *stay* with the Ispaklaria which is the *real* reality, you know, the one without the mask, and *you're going away* with this *virtual* reality here in my room."

"Look, I've got a little experience in this reality de-

KINGS AND CAMP COUNSELORS

partment, and . . . trust me, it's the same. And you're best off thinkin' of it like . . . like taking a little trip."

Elisha opened the bag. There was snack food, a Swiss army knife, a cellphone and he couldn't even tell what was at the bottom.

Aaron smiled. "Well, you might get hungry or need to make contact!"

Elisha didn't really want to take it, and didn't even want to ask Aaron where he had gotten the stuff from, but he was used to adults insisting on this type of thing, so he reluctantly put the knapsack on his back. It weighed on him like an unwanted sweater.

He sat down at his desk and looked suspiciously at Aaron. "Why are you wearing two whistles?"

"Oh, one's for you," he said, putting it over Elisha's head. "You know, this is like the buddy system, and in case our other communications fail, this hopefully won't," and he smiled ear to ear. He really was so proud of himself. He was making milestone breakthroughs in the 'letting go' department, milestones!

Elisha bit his lip nervously. Why was Aaron so gung-ho-looking all of a sudden? He was acting like one of those camp counselors who'd force you to jump into the black mucky lake when they wouldn't even set their big toes into it. Elisha sighed. The code probably wasn't even for the First Temple. It was too easy. *Too impossible.* He was probably headed for some underwater, alien-shark-infested prison cave 29,283,338 leagues under the sea in a black hole. Elisha stuffed Rav Kadosh's 'calling card' into the knapsack. Up until now it had seemed to work much better than any cellphone or whistle. Then he took a deep breath. Hadn't he always wanted to be an astronaut when he was little? Why did that seem like light-weight kid stuff right about now? Actually, he could just see getting his own memorial wall at school, maybe even a bigger one than they had for Ilan Ramon.

Aaron held the triangular-shaped Ispaklaria key in his hands and carefully placed the *Choshen* stone in the center. The blinding light-beams immediately shot out in every direction and Aaron's voice seemed too thrilled to Elisha when he said, "It's still workin' today!" He put on two pairs of sunglasses and then double-checked the printout from Elisha's father and added a firm, "Yup. It's *absolutely* still stuck on the kiddy-proofed line: 2928–3338." He winked at Elisha and said, "One 'T' it is!" and then excitedly motioned Elisha to stand in front of the mirror stone.

That's when Elisha felt his first full-blown panic attack. Was he really going to let a 40-something-year-old, insane homeless person train-wreck his life? Even if he was the 'Priest of Light'? It was the first time in Elisha's life that he *finally* understood that stupid sentence his father always liked to say. How did it go? Oh yeah, "If your friends jumped off a roof, would you jump too?"

"OK. Let's remember those ground rules Rav Kadosh told us." Aaron scratched his head. "What do you remember?"

"That I'm supposed to be selfless. Which I'm not yet . . ."

"Right, but no problemo, I've got enough selflessness for both of us this morning." Aaron started counting off on his fingers. "OK. One: Read the writin' on the wall—yours truly cracked that one already, so we're good—*check*. Two: Only in daylight—*check*. OK, we're ready."

Elisha groaned. "There was a lot more than just two things!"

KINGS AND CAMP COUNSELORS

"Well if we don't remember them, they probably weren't *that* important," Aaron said as he pointed the clear rainbow cylinder beam directly at the mirror stone while Elisha halfheartedly walked into the path of the rainbow light. Absolutely nothing happened. The mirror stone kept its usual rock-solid form with its flat light-blue surface. Aaron adjusted the direction and then said, "Okay, now together we're gonna try to align the key straight."

It happened so quickly that Elisha almost choked. The mirror's surface turned into a rushing waterfall, except the water was rushing up and it was only two inches in front of his face. He instantly became soaking wet and then his body felt like it was being forced out of a tight-neck bottle just when his whole room turned into a reflection. It was as if his room and Aaron had turned into the mirror stone—they were a two-dimensional mirror image and the Ispaklaria was a real three-dimensional place. The water*up* suddenly disappeared and there was an ominous gray whirlwind suddenly engulfing Elisha on every side. He was still on his feet, but now Aaron and his room were nowhere in sight.

Aaron was still in Elisha's room, checking that his right hand was okay. It was only his fingertips that had touched the water*up*, but he couldn't take his eyes off his hand. He was looking at a bare bony skeleton from his knuckles to his fingertips. There was no sensation of pain, but it hurt to just look at them. *That would have been warning number three.* He was supposed to leave the 'connectin' to the *Yessod* . . . .

Barely ten seconds had gone by, and Elisha was already desperate to be back in his normal room, even if it was flat and two-dimensional. His body was being battered by forceful gusts of wind from every direction, and he could barely keep his eyes open. There wasn't anything familiar that he could see, and he couldn't even move from the strength of the violent wind. The sound of his clothes and knapsack blowing was deafening. The Red Sox cap was long gone, and it felt like the whistle was choking him to death as it shrilled away in the wind. He wondered if he was in the middle of a cyclone. He was still clear-minded enough to realize that he was utterly insane for doing this. Fear was pounding through every inch of his body, when in the next instant everything stopped.

A thick fog replaced the noisy wind, and Elisha thought he was inside a massive cloud, but not a regular cloud. It was like his mind had shut down and he was in a grey space where all his senses were dead. He couldn't see, hear or speak, and he couldn't even feel, but inside he was screaming. He tried to reason with himself. Aside from the fact that he could still think, he was seriously wondering if he was dead. He certainly felt a sort of deadness. It was like he was hanging in limbo in a gray world. Was he just a soul, was this what happened when you died?

A scream rose from the depths of his mind, and it ignited a fire. In the flash of a second, all of Elisha's five senses came back, but stronger than he could ever remember them. He was in the middle of a fiery world, and with his heightened vision he could see the fire for miles. He could also hear every sizzle, crackle and explosion, and his body felt an acute burning sensation even though he wasn't on fire. The smell and taste of burning volcano was so strong that all of Elisha's senses felt overwhelmed. It was like super senses on fire that came along with terrible and bitter feelings of complete agony. Now he even wanted to die. He cried out. He was crying so hard that he almost missed the voice. The still small voice had come and was telling him to move toward the glow. It was a speaking silence. Elisha raised his eyes. There was a distinct glow around the fire. Maybe that was it? In his agitated state he willed himself to walk to the glow. The glow became golden, then lighter, and then formed into the shape of a corridor. There was an opening at the end, and he saw it clearly because there was bright white light seeping in. He rushed in the direction of the light.

The Foundation Vault was pitch black. It was darker than her own windowless room. It was darker than the solid black stones that went up to her circular ceiling. She left it. There was no reason to be there anymore. There was no more wisdom coming from the crack in the wall that led to infinity. Professor Bezalel was gone. There was no more Arranger of Letters. The *Yessod* had done that. Everyone was sleeping. Everyone was running around with little nothings in their somebody minds and stuck in their spots that were only a speck of dust in the universe.

The 17th of Tammuz had come and gone, and her 12th year in the Chambers didn't begin. The spot in time didn't happen. The *Yessod* didn't come. Not the first day. Not the second day. Not the third day. Not the fourth day. Not the fifth day. She knew she wasn't wrong about the days; she held time within her. Only the Princess of Sheba had come and gone today, and she was fighting against the days.

A tear dropped from her eye. She knew it was only a raindrop in the sea, one tiny piece of dust in the Supernal Universe.

She made her own pile of dust and then had it fill her room. The big people didn't like dust. They were always trying to get rid of it instead of thinking about it. She turned her dust into a spiral and watched for the special spots in time. She knew that the somebodies thought that *they* made the spots in time. They thought that if they decided a spot in time was happy or sad, then it became what they wanted. They were wrong. It was the opposite. The moon and sun calendar had spots in time that would shoot their way up through the whole spiral of time even until infinity and force all the days to be exactly the way they were created to be. There were spots in time for resting, spots for starting again, spots for fixing, spots for feeling sorry, spots for being happy and spots for dancing, spots for light, spots for trees, spots for freedom, spots for learning, and one spot for crying and losing that had to share its spot with winning.

She forced her dust to travel at the speed of light and watched time stand still. The past, present and future were now all One. That only worked with dust. You couldn't change time. You couldn't change waiting. You couldn't change the spots. You could do everything if you were no thing in the Supernal Universe, but you couldn't change the illusion of time in the Eighth Kingdom. That's why she had been waiting for the *Yessod*, because the *Yessod could*.

After running straight through a wall of solid lightning, Elisha found himself standing not in some fantastic and amazing place, but in a very, very familiar spot. He looked behind him and saw there was a dark shadow-cloud suspended in mid-air in the exact shape of his own mirror stone. Elisha turned to the side. Why couldn't he place this spot? He studied the view in front of him. He *knew* this view. The hills, the type of trees, but something was definitely entirely different. It was then that he understood! He must have walked right outside his own front door, but it definitely, definitely didn't look the way it did now. He quickly turned around to search for what he was sure would be his main point of reference . . . but he never got the chance. In a second there was a coarse cloth sack around his entire body. He started flailing his arms wildly, screaming and punching in the air. Of all things, he was being captured or kidnapped after nearly dying. He felt completely helpless. All his physical efforts were completely worthless too; there were at least two men out there, and they felt as strong as iron. His captors started speaking to each other.

"Thou shalt follow the King's command, even if terror grippeth thy right hand."

Elisha felt instantly relieved. He wasn't sure if it was just the relief of understanding that this 'ultimate reality' place had speaking human beings, or if it was because they were speaking Hebrew and he could understand every word. It was a strange Hebrew though. No, it was actually Biblical Hebrew. The men seemed to be arguing. From his muffled bag world, Elisha started concentrating on their low keyed conversation.

"Nay. This is no child, Benaiah, this is Ashmodai himself. A demon, that we shall slay ourselves and spare our noble King the discomfort."

Elisha almost choked on their words. His First Temple 'reality' was already his last. He felt himself being lifted up onto a horse and then heard a sword being drawn. The other voice warned: "The mighty King hath clearly spoken that thou shalt not uproot a single hair from his head."

The first voice now sounded restrained: "Fear not, Benaiah. I am not the betrayer of your will or his. I shall follow the King's command despite my sound reasoning and shall swiftly take him to the palace."

"Nay, Azariah. The King will see him in his meditation chamber."

Elisha could barely believe his ears. He was going to be taken to a *king,* and certainly a meditation chamber sounded a lot better than a torture chamber. All he could think about now was, *which* king was he about to see? He felt his heart exploding with unbearable curiosity. He had never paid much attention in class when Professor Bezalel wasn't his teacher, but he did remember that most of the kings were *really* nasty and wicked during the 400 years that the First Temple stood, so he'd better hope for the best. There was a loud whack, and the horse started off at top speed. There were lots of turns, but barely three minutes later he was lifted off the horse and then dropped onto a hard surface. His captor quickly cut a hole in the bag with his sword and ran off. Elisha took it as a sign that he could emerge. He carefully stepped out of the sack and studied his surroundings. He froze.

He had never seen a more wondrous sight in his whole entire life. He was inside a room with absolutely gigantic proportions, some kind of royal chamber with a massive foyer, where the ceiling, floor and walls were made entirely out of polished aquamarine. Elisha had a sudden realization that his mirror stone was somehow a teeny square chip from this room. It seemed impossible, and yet this entire colossal sanctuary seemed to be made all out of *one* continuous aquamarine gem. It was like a

KINGS AND CAMP COUNSELORS

crystal-clear ocean and a perfect sky together. There was such an intense beauty and brilliance assaulting his senses that Elisha felt more humble than he had ever felt in his entire life. But in the center of the room was a sight that dwarfed everything else.

His eyes became totally fixated. He was looking at a huge throne and it seemed to be in mid-air. There were four-winged creatures of extraordinary beauty on each side with different faces—a human, a lion, an eagle and an ox. They seemed to be in flight, and their faces seemed four-dimensional, if that was possible. Elisha rubbed his eyes, but he could still see their faces in a panoramic 360 degrees all at once—he could see the front, left and right side and also the top and back of each of their heads, even though he was only looking at them from the front. Elisha knew it was something he probably shouldn't even be looking at —a replica of the *Merkavah* from the Book of Ezekiel. And Professor Bezalel had warned them that the *Merkavah* was one of the deepest and most complicated Kabbalah secrets that exist. Any study of the *Merkavah* would be off-limits to him until he either turned 40 or became a Chamber Seven graduate. Elisha was not even 11, but he understood that this sight was an overwhelming gift. His eyes quickly shifted to the corner of the room where an intense glow of light was moving his way. The light-form went in front of the *Merkavah*-like throne. It seemed at first to be a blurry hologram, but the image slowly sharpened into the form of a person. And not *just* a person. It only took a second for Elisha to find himself bowing all the way down to the floor. Instinctively he knew that he wouldn't dare look up until he was told. The voice in front of him spoke an elegant Hebrew that sounded like beautiful music.

"You may rise."

Elisha slowly lifted his head, and the picture was one that he wanted embedded in his memory forever. There on the spectacular throne was a man that he could only describe as being in the image of the Divine. His countenance was smooth and glowing with kindness and wisdom, wisdom that you could feel. His face was framed with silver tresses as smooth as silk, and he had clear blue eyes that were intensely beautiful and matched the aquamarine room. Elisha was mesmerized and couldn't even blink. There was a glimmering gold and jeweled crown that was floating in fluid suspension above the King's head. Even his robes were a shade of purple that you can only see at sunset, and the color was changing with his every movement.

"Welcome Elisha, son of David. You are standing before Solomon, son of David, son of Jesse, King of Israel."

Elisha just couldn't speak. He was too shocked and was sure that his mouth was locked shut.

"You have come a long way, so please be seated."

Elisha didn't remember there being a chair, but as he sat down, one quickly appeared, and then a crystal-clear table was suddenly before him as well. The King pointed to his knapsack.

"May I?"

Elisha almost couldn't understand the request, but after the King motioned a second time, he eagerly brought his knapsack to him, still stunned and still not able to speak a word. The King unzipped the bag and started taking things out. In this completely strange place, Elisha suddenly realized just how weird his own stuff would look. To Elisha's astonishment, the King pulled out one item at a time and studied each one while placing them on the crystal table.

"Hmm, what do we have here? A Swiss army knife, primitive cellphone, post-it parchment . . ."

Primitive? Elisha wondered to himself.

The King was now pulling out a bag of potato chips. Elisha was sure that this one had stumped the King. He held it up to the light and then quickly said, "Oh yes, junk food. And what else . . . well, well, well, Coca Cola, the real thing. Would you mind?"

Elisha was so speechless that he hoped that he had at least nodded the answer.

But he seemed happiest with Rav Kadosh's 'calling card', which was actually a small book of *Tehillim*.

"Now this is truly special. My father would have been delighted to see his Psalms in print and in miniature, especially embedded with such an advanced global positioning system."

The King's face seemed to just be shining with happiness and gentleness. All Elisha could think was that he could easily spend the rest of his life just sitting speechless in the glow of this great man.

"How nice of the *Kohen Gadol* to have packed these things for me."

The word '*Gadol*' was not lost on Elisha. He had clearly called Aaron the '*High*' priest, *not* just priest, and Elisha would remember it.

"If it is not too much trouble, could you please ask him next time for a set of Talmud, the Sepharad Sapir edition, for my personal studies, a digital camera, and, if at all possible, a laptop." The King laid a small beautiful diamond on the table. "That should suffice."

Elisha still couldn't find his vocal chords. All he could do was stare with his mouth open, although he guessed that he shouldn't have expected anything less from the man known as the wisest in the world. He motioned Elisha to pay attention. As if he could do anything else.

The King rose with his scintillating robes shining in every direction and said, "Behold my words, Elisha son of David, for I have used my mind to seek and probe by wisdom *all* that happens beneath the heavens. And now I shall impart some of my mind's experience and knowledge to *you*. For the beginning of wisdom is to *acquire* wisdom."

Elisha was following the King's every movement as he walked across the expanse of the aquamarine floor.

"And while I presume that this must all appear so very extraordinary to you, it is really quite *simple* from a physics point of view."

Elisha hadn't even started studying physics, but he was 100% determined at that moment to commit every single incomprehensible physics formula to memory.

The King scanned the massive room in silence. "Let us just say that we are quite close to the core of an energy superhighway—a meeting-point of the spiritual and physical universe. In fact, *all* the dimensions converge just minutes from here at the site of the *Even Hashtiyah*, the Foundation Stone, which is in essence a transit point for changing energy into matter." King Solomon's head motioned toward the area behind him and to the right— Mount Moriah, the Temple site. "And using my gift of wisdom, and an ever-so-slight adjustment of the Ispaklaria's space-time continuum, I was able to create some . . . let us just call them pre-set meeting points for us."

Elisha *thought* he 'got it.' The King had figured out how to time-travel.

KINGS AND CAMP COUNSELORS 41

The King looked at Elisha and smiled slightly, "Regrettably, time travel is obsolete science fiction. Woe to one who travels in their illusions rather than breaking them, for the only way to dispel the fourth dimension is by applying the fifth." He then stared at a point on the wall behind Elisha. "However, I am indeed in need of a slight technical adjustment. Therefore I must beseech you to move the Ispaklaria to the *east* side of your room, as that will afford direct access into my chambers, leaving only the illusion of time between us."

The King stopped alongside a colossal aquamarine pillar which reflected his long robes like a kaleidoscope. "There are 2,824 years separating us in the illusion of time. Look at your digital watch, Elisha. You will never be able to be in my space-time continuum for more than 18 minutes or, I am sorry to say, you will disintegrate and your energy will return to The Source. Use your time wisely, especially when the *time* comes. And may the Master of the Universe who is the Ultimate Timeless Reality, hasten it in its time."

Elisha felt like his mind was spinning with information, and yet he could effortlessly remember every detail that the King was saying. The King was now moving closer to him.

"You have already deciphered that there are five dimensions of nothingness on your key. However, you shall *only* use the fourth, the illusion of time, until I shall order otherwise. For there is a *time* for everything," the King smiled knowingly. "Moreover, *our* spiral alignment window is limited to a period of precisely 38 days in the year, from the first of the month of Tammuz to the 9th of the month of Av. You have delayed your visit by 23 days, and there are only 15 days left. And it is a wise son who harvests in the summer." The King clapped his hands and said, "You must return now. Do not mind my men, they will not harm you." The King seemed ready to go, but then he slowly turned back.

"You may not see the Temple right now. Do *not* even try. Her glory will blind you in your present state. Alas, only *you* can adjust your selflessness. But do return directly. There is much that I must teach you. Two years is really so little time for the task at hand."

With that, King Solomon was gone and the guards returned with the sack. This time Elisha didn't resist. He understood why and even longed for the comfort of a dark bag with no sensory stimulation. His wild thoughts were more than overwhelming on their own.

They released him right near the dark shadow of his mirror stone that was still hanging like a cloud in mid-air. It was a huge effort not to take a quick peek over his shoulder in the direction of the Temple, and the dark shadow wasn't particularly inviting. The very thought of having to go through volcanoes and tornadoes practically paralyzed his whole body with fear. But it wasn't like he had any choice. It was that or go back to 'The Source.'

With a deep breath and squared shoulders, Elisha touched the cloudy looking Ispaklaria, desperately hoping his room would instantly reappear. It did, but in the flat state of a mirror image, and everything was only a two-dimensional reflection, including Aaron. Then he found himself in the middle of the Ispaklaria, looking back as if it was a window. In that direction the view was three-dimensional. At least out there it *looked* real. He turned around and tried knocking on Aaron's reflection. Suddenly he felt himself exploding out of the tight-necked bottle again.

KINGS AND CAMP COUNSELORS

Aaron seemed upset to see him and kept looking at his own hands.

"Well, this is never goin' to work if you don't even try!"

"WHAT! Are you kidding?!" Elisha was beside himself with indignation, and he also realized that those were the first words that came out of his mouth since he'd left eighteen minutes ago. "You mean you didn't see what happened?!"

"In one second?" Aaron scoffed.

Elisha looked at his watch. 18 minutes had definitely passed. He held his watch right in front of Aaron's face. Aaron became confused and then seemed stunned and double-checked his own watch.

"Hey! What? Well . . ." He massaged his jaw and said, "You know, I was thinkin' that you did kind of flatten out like one of those cut-out cardboard ads, but I thought it was because I was wearin' two pairs of sunglasses." Aaron whipped them both off and then stared down at his hands. "Or maybe losin' my finger-flesh traumatized me." He exercised his fingers and then puckered in his cheeks while looking at Elisha in the strangest way.

"What's the matter?" Fear gripped Elisha, maybe he was turning skeletal too.

"No. You're fine. It's just that you've got . . . I don't know how to describe it, but—well—just turn around and take a look."

Elisha inspected himself and was pleasantly relieved to see that all his skin and flesh were still intact. But there were also little skinny silvery rays shooting out of his pores, which, even as he watched, were fading fast. Aaron was watching too while urgently pressing him, "Well, go on. *What happened*?!"

Elisha related to Aaron in full detail how he had spent those bizarre 18 minutes. Aaron could barely believe the part about the camera and laptop, but it actually didn't outrank anything else on his 'let go' meter. Elisha felt that the biggest snag would be rearranging the furniture in his room, but other than that he was on a high. It was as if he had been suddenly transformed into the most important person on the face of the earth, which he was sure did nothing for his selflessness. But by the time some of his burning excitement had worn off, he felt like killing himself. Here he had just spent at least ten minutes with none other than King Solomon, and he hadn't asked a single question. What had he actually accomplished to help understand why any of this was happening? So much for using his time wisely . . . but, he *could* see him again, couldn't he? That was amazing! He could barely wait for tomorrow.

But then like a thud of weighted heaviness, deep sleep became the only thing on Elisha's mind. His whole body was aching, and an overwhelming sense of exhaustion hit him. He suddenly felt that he *had* to rest right now.

Aaron was the complete opposite: "Come on, Elisha. We've got a royal shoppin' list to take care of."

There was nothing that Elisha would rather do than to get the things to the King as quickly as possible, but it was absolutely impossible. He felt like he could barely move. His whole body was collapsing. He had to sleep, and he had to sleep *now*. He practically begged Aaron with a yawn,

"Could you please do it? I want to, but I'm too tired."

Aaron hesitated. He should probably wait and go

KINGS AND CAMP COUNSELORS

with Elisha, but he blurted his thoughts out loud, "Listen, you gotta remember that I'm a workin' man as of tomorrow mornin'. So, it's either today or forget it!"

Elisha was fading fast, "Just take the diamond and sell it, and I'm going to take a tiny little nap and then . . ."

Aaron never heard the last words, because Elisha had said them in his sleep. Aaron couldn't help feeling a bit worried. Elisha was that delicate-looking type of boy, and in those last seconds before he fell asleep he seemed almost flimsy. The 'trip' did sound like a physical nightmare. That's probably why only a kid's body could handle the abuse. He double-checked his own perfectly fine fingertips and thought, *kids are resilient. He'll be bouncin' back after a little nap.*

CHAPTER THREE

Long Term Investments

**A TIME TO SCATTER STONES
AND A TIME TO GATHER STONES**

Aaron had no problem selling the jewel. He walked away from the diamond district with 100,000 shekels in cash and was sure by the generous way he was handed the bills that he had gotten ripped off. He couldn't have cared less. He was flying high. Even in the best of times, Aaron never had so much money in the bank, never mind in his own wallet. He also had wisely gone into Tel Aviv where he didn't know a soul, but the hitch was that he also didn't know his way around. Only the fourth person he asked could give him decent directions to the mall. He also realized that he missed having Elisha along for the field trip. But there was no way he was going to wait with this mission. After all, Elisha had told him he was the *High* Priest, and that apparently came with shopping responsibilities.

Aaron studied the mall index and decided to buy the digital camera first, *and* to enjoy every minute of a 'let gooooo' shopping spree.

"I'd like the best digital camera money can buy,"

Aaron said as he confidently walked up to the counter. The store owner's eyes brightened.

"Very well, except that some of these more state-of-the-art ones can be confusing to operate. Is the camera for you?"

Aaron couldn't help himself, "No. It's for King Solomon."

The store owner groaned inwardly while faking a laugh. The richest customers always seemed to have the worst sense of humor . . . "Well, then, take the Futura 890ZX. It's got every feature possible, and *he* should be able to figure it out."

Aaron went in search of the laptop next. He walked self-assuredly into a sleek-looking high-tech store and scanned the display shelves. He couldn't figure out a thing. All the computers looked the same, just different sizes, and there were no salesmen to be seen. He really needed Elisha for this one. Then he heard some arguing in the back room. It sounded like the boss was upset. A skinny teenager wearing a bright orange and yellow BigByte vest emerged looking completely depressed. Aaron was happy to be the one to make his day.

"I'm lookin' for your best laptop, somethin' king-sized, but I gotta tell you, I don't know the first thing about 'em."

The smile on the kid's face almost looked like a cry. He showed Aaron the most expensive one in the store. When Aaron saw the price his mouth dropped open, so BigByte kid quickly told him, "You can pay it in 36 installments."

Yeah, like car installments, thought Aaron. But the best meant nothing less.

Aaron was still counting out the bills when the kid

ran into the back room practically shouting, "A Pentiluxe K900M, in cash!"

Aaron left the store feeling a surge of self-satisfaction, but then couldn't remember how to get out of the mall. He was searching for the exit signs when he spotted skinny kid's photo being placed as 'Employee of the Month' in the store window.

Yoram smiled at Jonathan. "Five hours ahead of your deadline. Nice. Are you trying to set a new record, 'cause it's not going to earn you a raise."

Jonathan smiled back. "I'll settle for diversity instead. Switch me to the Knesset for a bit."

Jonathan's editor laughed. "At your age?"

"Then give me the Prime Minister's office."

"Right—just keep setting your sights higher."

"Then at least City Hall."

"That's veteran territory."

"You mean senior citizen, and that's why you haven't had a front page scandal in over a decade."

"Gee, and I thought it was because we finally have some honest politicians in office."

Jonathan stared straight into his editor's eyes and then wasn't surprised when he scribbled something out on a piece of paper and handed it to him.

"I'm giving you one day to prove yourself. I want an article in my inbox in 24 hours."

It was just what Jonathan had wanted—a ticket to start rubbing shoulders with the politicians, the power brokers. True, Tel Aviv's City Hall was small fry, but it was a good enough place for Jonathan to get his feet wet and see if it offered an entertaining enough career for a soon-to-be Chamber Seven graduate.

He returned to his cubicle to gather up some notes before heading out to City Hall. While there, he also logged into the newspaper's central data repository, hoping to find something that would shed light on his strange symptoms. He couldn't help hanging onto a thread of denial. Maybe there was some logical explanation *other* than *tohu v'bohu*. He found a mountain of clinical research suggesting that delirium could be a side effect of amateur hypnosis, along with mild hallucinations and panic attacks. It didn't make Jonathan feel any easier. He just felt cornered into a catch-22. If he could regain his Chamber Seven empowerment, he'd obviously get rid of his *tohu v'bohu*. BUT first he needed his Chamber Seven *memories*. So it was either back to hypnosis with Dr. Brody, who might have given him the *tohu v'bohu* to begin with—or *not*. He stared at the three words flashing across his home page. 'Taekwondo Qualification Tournament.' *She knows how to get into the Foundation Vault. She does.* How could she possibly resist him when she once worshipped the ground he walked on? Well, at least she did before that loser Akiva came along. It certainly wasn't Jonathan's fault that he had totally forgotten about her.

A searing determination came over him. Devorah Barak was it—a full set of keys. She could save him from *tohu v'bohu*, open up the Foundation Vault, and help him unlock the 9th of Av. She'd also be a nice little trophy to celebrate his personal triumph. *Win-win-win*.

Aaron's last stop was for the set of Talmud. But there were no religious book stores in the mall. He didn't know the area and kept asking passersby if they knew where he could find one. Finally, an extremely tall Chassid pointed him in the right direction and gave him very complicated directions, adding, "It's really only two minutes from here."

Aaron found it after fifteen, and it was more like a hole in the wall than a storefront. The entrance was a very narrow glass door that sported enough ripped-off stickers to be opaque and had a handwritten cardboard sign that read: "Moshe's Trading Post. Old and New Books Sold." Aaron frowned. He really didn't think the King should have anything second-hand, but having come this far he figured he would give it a try. The door opened with the loudest creak Aaron had ever heard.

The 'store' was actually a narrow hallway, and it felt even narrower because it was filled two stories high with books all the way up to the vaulted ceiling. The odor of mildew and dust was so heavy you could just about feel it. Way in the back, a kindly-looking, *very* old store owner was drinking tea. He didn't even notice Aaron coming in. Finally Aaron coughed as loud as he could, but there was still no reaction. Aaron was sure that the man must be deaf, and he was about to leave when the store owner spoke up.

"How may I help you, young man?"

Aaron was doubtful, but pulled out the small piece of paper where he had written down the edition that the King had requested.

"I'm lookin' for a Sapir Sepharad set of Talmud."

The storeowner looked shocked. "The Sapirs have been out of print since my bar mitzvah!"

Aaron's whole face dropped in disappointment. Judging by the store owner's age, that must have been at least seventy years ago. Now it was the store owner's

LONG TERM INVESTMENTS 51

turn to be curious.

"And the *Sepharad* edition of the Sapirs *never* was in print. It disappeared almost a thousand years ago." He squinted his eyes suspiciously at Aaron and demanded, "Who sent you here?!"

Aaron wasn't in the mood to answer 'King Solomon' and certainly didn't want to seem disrespectful, so he kept silent. But the store owner's voice was now becoming urgent.

"What's your name, young man?!" he demanded as his face flushed red.

Aaron was overcome by a deep desire to run out of the store, but he didn't want to upset the old man even more. And heck, when was the last time someone referred to him as a young man? So he answered, "Aaron Kohen."

The store owner was now smiling from car to ear and was very excited. He started speaking very fast. "Well, that's a very good name indeed! Yes, it is, indeed it is, my dear Kohen, yes, Mr. Aaron Kohen, very good!"

Aaron was now sure that the man was loony tunes, and without trying to hurt his feelings he slowly turned to the door and kindly said, "Well, thank you for your help anyways."

"What, you're leaving?! I wouldn't dream of it, leaving without your set of *Sepharad* Sapirs. I wouldn't hear of it!"

Now it was Aaron's turn to be even more confused. "But, but I thought you said that it's out of print."

"Yes, yes it *is* out of print." The storeowner now gave him a very precise wink, "But you can even have my very own set which was passed down for tens of generations and which I received on the very date of *my* bar mitzvah if . . . if you know what I mean," he said with his eyebrows raised.

"Oh, Aha." Aaron now knew precisely what he meant. So this had all been salesmen tactics. Well, then he'd have no problem playing along. He'd pay the man whatever he wanted if he would part with his dearly-beloved ancient bar-mitzvah present. "Just name your price!"

It was the wrong thing to say. The elderly store owner turned furious.

"Young man, you must be crazy. It's priceless!"

Aaron was already regretting having set foot in the store. The man was clearly not okay upstairs, and as badly as he felt for him, he really needed to be moving on.

The store owner now positioned himself in front of the door. "I don't want money. I want the password!"

Great, thought Aaron, *now I can't even get out of this hole without knowing a password.*

The store owner was adamant, and Aaron was at a total loss what to do. He certainly wasn't going to use force to move the elderly man away from the door. *Okay,* he thought to himself, *I'll play the game.* He wondered what kind of password he should blurt out . . . *Rumpelstiltskin, Supercalifragilisticexpialidocious, Bishop to Knight 3,* but it was obvious that the elderly store owner was desperate to help him out. He was staring in anticipation with his wide cataract-bleared eyes and nodding his head as if the password was already uttered. Aaron just stood there clueless.

"Well, young man *what* is it??"

"Uh, could you maybe just give me a tiny little hint here?"

The man's face shadowed over with a lifetime of disappointment.

LONG TERM INVESTMENTS   53

"Never mind. Sorry, but this set is spoken for. It actually has been for hundreds and hundreds of years."

"Well then could you please just tell me where else I could get one?"

The old man's laugh would have sounded hysterical if it wasn't so pained.

"It is obvious, young sir, that you not only know very little about sacred books, but you know absolutely nothing at *all* about the *Sepharad* Sapir Talmud. *IF* there even exists another *Sepharad* on earth, you'd probably have to break into the Vatican to find it!"

That last line couldn't help making an impression on Aaron. If any of this somehow was true, he might just be giving up on his only chance to secure the King's wishes. Aaron stared boldly into the old man's face and decided to play it straight.

"Look, you're right, I don't know a thing about Sapir Talmud. But I promise you, sir, that I am on an important mission for one of the most important people in the world, and I just *have* to have that set!"

The elderly man was unfazed. "Well if it's *so* important to you, then you'll have to try a bit harder to remember *who* sent you. The code name I mean." And with that his eyes lit up in anticipation once again. "You know, the alias name . . ."

It was clear that the elderly man was somehow coaxing him on. Aaron started racking his brains. Maybe there was some connection, maybe this crazed old lunatic wanted somehow to hear the truth. What would King Solomon's code name be? Most probably 'Kohelet' or 'Ecclesiastes,' the name he'd given himself in his famous book. There was nothing to lose, so he said it.

The storeowner stared at him in utter disbelief.

"THAT'S IT! That's it! Good. *Excellent!!*" The man was grinning now from ear to ear and tripling the wrinkles in his face. "Now, *who* is sleeping??" And with that he managed a wink out of his protruding eyes.

This whole thing was utterly bizarre, but Aaron felt he was on a roll, and he certainly was going to keep going with it.

"Um. Elisha?"

"Full name, please."

"Elisha Davidson."

The storeowner now seemed as excited as a young boy. He was mumbling all kinds of words to himself, and then in a loud and trembling voice he said, "*Unbelievable!* Who would have thought it was true!" He then slid over a very tall ladder and pointed to a low-ceilinged loft high above the bookshelves. "The set is right up there in the far back, young man. It's been waiting there just for *you.*"

Waiting a few centuries, thought Aaron, but certainly the elderly man wasn't going to go up on the ladder and pull them down. Oh yes, but he was, and he was going to continue to mumble while each step took two minutes.

"Why you young-generation people can't complete a full sentence, though, is beyond me. Would it have been so difficult to say the password the right way?"

That piqued Aaron's curiosity, so he couldn't help asking, "And what would have been the *right* way?"

The old man turned slowly around on the ladder and spread his hands wide for effect, and then his voice boomed out dramatically:

> "The Sepharad Sapirs are for safekeeping
> Until the day that *Kohelet* is seeking,
> Aaron Kohen will be beseeching,
> While Elisha Davidson is sleeping."

He dropped the dramatic manner and grimaced at Aaron, "Now. Would that have been so difficult to say? *That* is what has been passed down for generations in our family of *Mekubalim* as the password. A nice *rhyming* password. Why couldn't you have made it rhyme, young man?" he asked, disgruntled, while starting to climb up another rung. "We have been sentries for centuries just waiting for that password, young man, and you couldn't even say it in rhyme."

Aaron just stared at him with an apologetic face, "Do you want me to do it now?"

"No, the magic of the moment has been totally ruined."

But *how weird* was all Aaron could think, and how far from a coincidence could all this be? And there was NO way he was going to spend a week to get a hold of those books. He thought he was going to have an impatience stress attack because the old man was only two rungs up after five minutes. Thankfully, he let Aaron take over, and then it only took ten minutes to get the set down. They were carefully stored away and perfectly preserved in three massive heavy oak trunks. But it took another 15 minutes just to clean off the thick coat of dust on the outside, and the small hallway store had turned into a grey cloud in the process. Aaron tried between sneezes to convince the store owner to accept money before he left, but he emphatically refused.

"What, are you insane, young man?!" he barked.

That was a good one, thought Aaron as he looked down at the three solid wood trunks. They *were* heavy, but kid stuff. Even the store owner was amazed to see how easily Aaron lifted up all three trunks and carried them out the door.

But once out on the street Aaron had regrets. He certainly couldn't start *schlepping* all of his purchases from bus stop to bus stop. He turned back to the small shop, but it was already closed! Not only that, but there was a sign on the door: "Closed for Good. The Beginning of Days has Arrived." Crazy till the end, thought Aaron. Just as he was wondering how he was going to get around, he remembered the fat wad of bills still in his wallet. He had at least 60,000 shekels left. Aaron patted the dust off his shoulders and smiled. *Now what would Donald Trump do in such a situation?* He straightened himself up and quickly hailed a cab.

The taxi driver was more than delighted to make the big-fare ride all the way to Jerusalem, but when he saw all the boxes and trunks he told him, "No way. You want me to order you the limo van service?"

"Sure."

After a comfortable hour's ride with DVD features and great AC, the limo van reached the Old City parking lot, and Aaron couldn't help groaning to himself. The Old City's scenic stone-paved narrow streets were closed off to cars and busses, which meant he'd have to walk the rest of the way with his over-sized and overweight load. There's nothing he hated more than a moving job in the Old City. Aaron told the driver to keep the meter running. He had no choice but to try and take all three trunks at once—the freebie *Sapirs* were just *too* valuable. If the driver made off with the laptop and camera it wouldn't be the worse loss. But then Aaron decided he wasn't going to take any chances and asked the driver to stack the laptop and camera on top. He then stalwartly moved forward

LONG TERM INVESTMENTS

with his load while onlookers marveled at his strength as he carried all three trunks at once without using a cart.

By the time Aaron reached the Davidsons' courtyard, he was so soaked with sweat he looked like he had taken a shower with his clothes on. He unloaded and then quickly went into the house to make sure the coast was clear before bringing in all the suspicious-looking trunks.

To Aaron's disappointment, the kid was still asleep. It must have been *some ride,* he thought to himself, but at least the house was empty.

He set all the trunks and packages down by the mirror stone, and that's when it *hit him!* There was a number *four* warning from Rav Kadosh, and it was a biggie! Elisha could end up with some kind of perpetual unconsciousness if he overdid his connectin'. *What had he called it?* Something like Snow White or Mulan or whatever sleeping disturbance . . . Aaron felt a rising panic as he tried to wake Elisha up. He wasn't responding!! Aaron started shaking him harder and harder. Elisha's body was limp and lifeless in his hands. Aaron could have kicked himself—*now what, now WHAT?* Cold water! He brought a whole bucket and emptied it over Elisha. *Nothing!* Why *hadn't* he seen the signs?? It was his lousy memory!! He had entirely forgotten about Rav Kadosh's warning!! Aaron was beside himself with the horrifying realization that was ripping through his gut. Why *hadn't* he remembered about that perpetual sleeping side effect?? Maybe CPR? Aaron barely hesitated.

"WHAT ARE YOU DOING TO ME!!"

Elisha was pushing Aaron's wet hand off his pinched nose with all his strength. Aaron let out a huge sigh of relief and then collapsed onto the wet bed. He was still breathing heavily.

"*Whew*!! That was a *close one*!" he stammered while still trying to catch his breath.

Elisha felt totally disoriented. *What was going on? What time was it? Why was he soaking wet?* Everything came back to him in a second when he saw the laptop and camera boxes piled high on top of three huge trunks. Elisha jumped out of bed, slipped right across the wet floor, and bumped his head on the wall.

Aaron just watched and said, "Thank God you're *okay* now. You nearly scared me half to death!"

"*Okay?*"

Aaron blew out heavily again, "Didn't think you'd *ever* wake up!"

Elisha rubbed his sore head and then his nose and looked at the large puddle of water on the floor. Aaron looked at it too and said, "Hey watch it, the water's going to get all this expensive stuff wet." He got up and started kneading the stress out of his shoulders and then wiped his forehead. "Come on, get changed and let's clean this up."

Elisha blurted out, "I don't like having all these things hanging around my room."

Aaron didn't like it any better. Elisha's parents were sure to be suspicious, and you couldn't easily explain away thousands of shekels' worth of purchases by a 10-year-old kid or a former beggar. But the Sapirs worried Aaron the most—if the other set was really in the Vatican, Mr. Davidson would probably know in a second.

Now Elisha understood why Rav Kadosh had warned him not to use the Ispaklaria more than once a day. He was still totally wiped out, but his mind was thinking sharply enough to come up with a plan. They had less than an hour before his mother came home. He

LONG TERM INVESTMENTS 59

asked Aaron to help him rearrange his bedroom. Elisha knew he'd have no problem moving the ten-ton Ispaklaria to the east side of his room. For some reason, he was the only one who could move it. But it meant first rearranging all the other furniture—a heavy chest of drawers, a four-door closet, a desk and a bed. Elisha smiled at Aaron's hulking frame. There were definite advantages to having a 'High Priest' who was also a professional mover.

"Remind me why we're doin' this again?" Aaron asked under the weight of the closet.

"King Solomon said this would be like a direct connection. I'm almost sure he meant that once we do this, I won't have to go through the tornado, fog and volcano worlds again and can just walk right into his chambers."

Elisha instinctively knew that Aaron could even handle the delivery himself. He just had to hold the Ispaklaria key and load the boxes and trunks to the other side. Aaron remembered his skeleton fingertips from the morning, but the plan seemed good enough as long as he didn't have to put any other body parts through.

The load easily disappeared through the water*up,* and to their relief it was out of Elisha's bedroom. Aaron was smiling even though he had a set of boney skeleton joints instead of hands.

"Not a bad way to get rid of unwanted stash!"

Now all that was left was a fat envelope with the leftover change from the diamond. But as small as the package was, it wouldn't go through the water*up*. Elisha was too tired to be bothered about something so hideable. He was exhausted again and wanted to head back to bed, but he snapped to attention, along with Aaron, when they heard the front door closing and his mother calling out, "I'm home."

Tamar Davidson came straight into the room, holding onto the arm of one of her favorite special ed students—Robert, who was autistic and blind. It *was* Monday. And that meant Robert would be staying for dinner.

His mother instantly noticed the change. "So, that's what you've been doing all day! But, you know what, I like it."

Gila pushed her way into the room. Elisha grimaced. He wasn't in the mood for Shira's annoying babysitter. She pulled Shira's hands away from her face so she could have a better look. "Honestly? I think it looked much better before."

Elisha threw her a fake smile and then his mother quickly added, "We're off to the supermarket. Come on Elisha, let's go."

Elisha looked like he couldn't budge. He hated going to the supermarket with Robert, even though he knew that's why his mother needed him with her. Aaron was giving him a get-your-act-together look from the side. Elisha yawned and stretched and then reluctantly parted ways with Aaron, who went straight to the computer.

Before he left, Aaron looked at him with some concern. "You're gonna be okay?"

"Yeah, I'm fine, just exhausted."

"*Again?*"

By suppertime Elisha was well into a full-force 'Sleeping Beauty' relapse. He kept drifting off at the table, even after Robert almost knocked him off his chair and even after his father announced that he still hadn't deciphered the last set of text symbols they had brought to his office. That set his father off. Jesse Davidson set down his fork and knife and asked, "Elisha, did you even hear what I just said?"

LONG TERM INVESTMENTS   61

Aaron had heard every word. He couldn't believe that Jessie was still trying to crack the last group of Ispaklaria symbols. It had been Aaron's idea to get the strange symbols decoded at the library, without of course ever telling Jessie where they came from. They had brought him all 12 lines of symbols, and the library's 'semiotics' program had worked like a dream until it crashed after unencrypting only seven of them. Well, it didn't seem like they really needed the last five anyways. They were doing pretty good without 'em. He just hoped that there was nothing *too* strange in there that would rouse Jessie's suspicions. Otherwise, he'd be breathing down his neck again to find out where the symbols came from.

"I would appreciate if you could *at least* give me some minimal respect and pay attention when I'm talking to you."

Elisha instantly straightened up and apologized, but couldn't help thinking that no one would even bother saying something like that to Robert. His father moved on to talking about a new project that as Head Librarian he had initiated with Elisha's school. It was going to be called the "Young Hebrew Literature Archives Institute." Aaron pretended to be highly interested, but Elisha just couldn't focus. He finally gave up and honestly asked if he could be dismissed because he was tired. His mother's face showed concern while she checked her watch in between feeding Robert.

"It's only 7:30. Are you feeling all right?"

His father took over and sternly asked, "What were you doing all day?"

Aaron decided to intercept while passing over the salad bowl; he couldn't let Elisha say that he was *sleeping*. "He's fine. He was just out playin' ball for six hours straight in the sun, and I think it got to him."

Elisha groaned. It was a bad save . . . .

His father set down his fork and said with an edge to his voice, "Well, now that you've wasted your entire day in idiotic pursuits, why should your evening be any different?"

Tamar was immediately upset by this comment and sent her husband a steely glare. Aaron could tell she was just waiting to have a stab. He picked up the cue, quickly wiped a napkin across his face, and followed Elisha down the hallway. That added to Jessie's annoyance, and now he was watching them both carefully and suspiciously. In seconds, Aaron could hear conjugal bickering starting up in the background.

"Did you find a child psychiatrist yet that passes your bar?!" Tamar asked in a sharp voice.

"No. Not yet . . ."

"Fine then, just keep putting it off, because now, on top of his nightmares, he's even wetting his bed!"

"*What?*"

"You heard me. I found his sheets soaking wet this afternoon.

Jessie lowered his head. "All right, fine. I'll take care of it."

Aaron watched with concern as Elisha just slumped right into a sleeping position. "You've got to snap out of this Elisha, I think your parents are gettin' worried, and you know what, so am I. Maybe you did get a dwarf-type dose of that Cinderella sleepin' syndrome or somethin'. Do you think I should check all of this with Rav Kadosh?"

Elisha was adamant. "No! I'm fine. You see that I keep waking up. Just how else am I supposed to feel after going through 2,824 years in 18 minutes?!"

The kid had a point. And then Elisha sleepily remembered that the stone had to be covered at night. "Could you cover the stone?"

Just as Aaron readied the blanket, he became mesmerized. There was a vivid black and white strand of snake-like fire shooting out of the Ispaklaria.

Even in his exhausted state, Elisha shot up out of bed, "Aaron, be careful! This could be an extremely important message. This is sort of," and he stopped, because it wasn't, "like the very first message I got when I went to look for you." It actually wasn't even close, because this time everything in his room was absolutely normal and the letters were just gently dancing around in the air. But he still continued urgently, "We have to remember everything that's written, and even then it could take us a whole day just to figure it out. Last time, if it wasn't for Rav Kadosh, I wouldn't have even known what to do or how to find you."

Aaron quickly armed himself with a pen and paper. He wasn't going to miss a word. They both waited, staring without even blinking at the burning Hebrew script. It read:

Everything arrived safely. Thank you.

Aaron, please keep the change.

They both couldn't help laughing at just how unmysterious the message was. Aaron was down to a few hearty chuckles as he started draping a large blanket over the mirror stone, but then he started having a major laughing fit that was getting worse and worse. Elisha realized it *must* be the money. He didn't even know how much 'change' was left. Aaron was dancing around the room. He knew exactly what *he* was going to do with the money. He took it out of his wallet, kissed it in the air and winked at Elisha.

"Good night kiddo!"

CHAPTER FOUR

Optical Illusions

A TIME TO SEEK

The radio blared out that it was 7:00 a.m. and that it was going to be another sunny day. Jonathan hadn't slept in 24 hours but couldn't agree more. He had gotten in every interview he needed yesterday and spent the entire night perfecting Chamber Four: Animating objects. It was quick, safe and simple. Lock-down had worked like a dream. He might even wait until he was a full-fledged Six before contacting Devorah.

Jonathan gulped down his orange juice and then went back to writing his latest article on city hall corruption. He didn't touch his laptop because he didn't have to. He simply spoke the words and they were being typed out automatically for him. He grinned to himself, his own version of *voice activated typing*. At first he'd tried adjusting it so that he could type out his articles straight from his mind without having to use his voice, but it hadn't worked out right. It was too fast for the keyboard to keep up with, or there were too many disconnected thoughts mixed in the middle—like *I'm starving, my back's itchy, got to remember to buy cat food*—that would end up

OPTICAL ILLUSIONS 65

taking him twice as long to edit out. Typing straight from the mind had also led to some weird slip-ups, like the one he'd almost missed when he described Councilwoman Dalyan as being a staunch defender of women's rights and grotesquely overweight.

Jonathan glanced at the finished mistake-proof article on his screen and was totally satisfied with himself. It still amazed him how these amateur crooks in the mayor's office weren't even mildly sophisticated in the way they had 'mishandled' or rather *stolen* the taxpayers' money. Jonathan had stumbled onto it immediately, but then he had to remind himself that it was only because he had read the city councilwoman's mind that he was able to put all the pieces together. *Oh well, life is tough*, he thought, *and I'm going to be the youngest recipient of the 'Golden Ink' award for journalism in less than a month after this*. He sent off his article directly by e-mail to his editor without ever going near his laptop and then slouched comfortably onto the sofa and cleaned up his apartment without moving an inch. He looked up for a moment and was satisfied that everything from the dirty dishes to the floor was being scrubbed up spic and span. Now he could even fire nosey old Svetlana, who just pushed the dirt around while yapping about her children in different disintegrating Eastern European countries, as if he cared.

Jonathan settled into his sofa and then popped a bag of microwave popcorn in his own hands. This morning he was getting started on his own personal research project, because frankly, even after one day he found the politicians a snore.

He first surfed through the sports channels. He had to admit that sports held an attraction for him. Turning himself into the 'numero uno' soccer player in the world would have lots of strategic advantages, even besides the money and women. But . . . there was something a little too brainless and jock-y about it. He needed to think *bigger.* He fed Stripes without moving a muscle and then had to smile as she flew through the air with her paws outstretched in every direction.

"Why do you do that every time?" he laughed softly as he grabbed her out of the air. Nope. Sports wasn't it. He started surfing through all the movie channels and watched the lead actors carefully. Objectively speaking, he'd rate himself a 'ten.' Taking that into consideration, he'd only need about a milligram's worth of his new empowerment to become a mega model or movie star. But, what was the 'ultimate' picture? A mansion with a pool in Beverly Hills? A supermodel wife that he'd divorce after two years? An Oscar statuette? No. It just didn't have *lasting* substance. He looked down at Stripes. She was so tiny. Maybe it was the cockiness coursing through his veins or his stupendous success in mastering Chamber Four, because he felt more than ready to try a teeny-weeny Chamber Five permutation. He of course still wouldn't venture transforming her into something else . . . but changing her size, well, that was kid stuff— the intro to Chamber Five. He concentrated on the basic permutations, and only 15 minutes later Stripes was ten times her normal size. Jonathan smiled and switched channels again. Cooking . . . boring. He continued surfing while petting Stripes' enormous head. It was fun petting something so fuzzy and *big.* The only down side was that Stripes was taking up most of the sofa and was squishing him into the armrest. She was also making him really hot. A documentary program caught all of his attention. He started watching intently until he couldn't hear a thing over Stripes' loud purring. She sounded like a broken lawnmower. He silenced her, returned her to her normal size and then picked her up and put her in his lap. He moved back into the center of the couch and continued watching the History channel with keen interest. He had barely watched five minutes when he couldn't see his flat screen at all. There was a massive wall of fur in front of his face. Stripes was taking up the *whole* living room.

Three hours later, she was still gargantuan. He had been absolutely meticulous in reversing every single letter, every single vowel, every single breath, but *nothing worked!* Every piece of edible protein in the house was gone too. Jonathan didn't like the way she was looking at him either. He was just about to call Devorah when he felt himself freefalling from a skyscraper.

Elisha woke up with more energy than ever, and starving. But it was one of those off mornings when his father hadn't gone directly to work, and Elisha almost wanted to back up into his room when he saw him; it was his stomach that braved him on. When he reached the busy Davidson breakfast table, which was more like everyone scurrying around for a different bowl of cereal, he heard the big news. Everyone in the Old City was talking about last night's mystery millionaire. Apparently a very wealthy man had just handed out several thousand shekels to every panhandler at the *Kotel*.

"I heard Michael Goldman was in town, I'm sure it was him," said Elisha's father.

His mother was quick to interject, "Judy Zimmerman told me it was Steven Grantfield from Hollywood."

Elisha looked right at Aaron. He wasn't giving himself away for a second and Elisha had no doubt in his mind *who* the miracle man was, but he just couldn't believe what a straight face Aaron was keeping.

"Too bad I missed it," Aaron laughed.

Elisha sighed to himself. If Aaron was that good at playing it cool, he'd never get to some of those other *big* secrets that Aaron was certainly hiding so well. He also hadn't eaten his cereal fast enough in order to avoid his father, and he was now being pulled to the side.

Jessie Davidson glanced back at his wife and continued with a restrained voice, "Elisha, you can't just waste away your entire summer vacation playing with a *ball*. I'm really very disturbed by all of this. I know the Chambers were cancelled, but we had an arrangement, didn't we, that you would be studying for at *least* two hours every day. You haven't even *touched* any of the books that I gave you up until now."

Elisha had honestly and completely forgotten all about it. Who wouldn't? He had nothing to say for himself, but his father did.

"It's all I'm asking, and it's really very little." He handed him four new books. "You'll like these. They're all beginner histories of ancient languages."

Elisha reluctantly took them while his father added, "Do you know that at your age—"

"You finished reading the whole young adult section of the library," Elisha finished the sentence for him. But apparently his father didn't appreciate the right answer. His restrained voice took on an edge to it.

"That's *right,* Elisha, and if you don't have the discipline to do it yourself, I'll have to think of some kind of new arrangement. How about a private tutor? Would you like that?"

OPTICAL ILLUSIONS   69

Elisha kept looking at the books. He'd like that like a hole in the head.

His father forced a smile. "This is going to be your last day playing soccer *all* day this summer. Is that clear?" Jessie looked over his shoulder. Tamar was still observing him from the kitchen, and he was sure that he passed with flying colors. He turned to Aaron: "Shall we? I can give you some orientation before Menashe gets in?"

Aaron answered, "Yes siree."

Elisha couldn't help feeling stabbed in the back. Aaron didn't have to leave for another hour and a half! He had been sure that Aaron was going to stay home with him to use the Ispaklaria. He *needed* to see King Solomon again. There wasn't anything more important than that! He watched them leave feeling totally dejected.

As Jessie went off to work, he couldn't stop wondering just how he could get Elisha's young mind interested in *something, anything* that mattered. He was sure that was all his son really needed, and not some bogus child psychiatrist. Aaron was energetically walking alongside him and whistling away, apparently keen to start his new job, but for some reason, he seemed too happy to Jessie for just that.

Losing Aaron to work was a disaster as far as Elisha was concerned. He looked at his mirror stone with longing and total frustration. How was he ever going to get back during daylight hours with Aaron working full time and a house full of nosey people around by the time he got back? *Traitor.* And then there was that selflessness problem, which he really had *no* idea how to deal with.

"Knock, knock," Elisha's mother said as she entered his room. She had Shira in one hand and a pile of mismatched socks in a basket in the other. "Guess what?

Not only are you *not* going to be bored today, you've actually got something really important to do," she said mysteriously as she set the basket down on Elisha's bed.

Elisha was hoping she wasn't referring to the laundry.

His mother pulled a sock out of Shira's mouth. "Believe it or not, Principal Oholiov just called and guess what? He thinks that Professor Bezalel could be up for a visit *and* he's hand-picked just three boys from your class and he's going to take you there at 1:00. Isn't that wonderful?"

Elisha and his mother started automatically matching the socks, but Elisha didn't think it was wonderful. He would have preferred to block out the whole Professor Bezalel business, and what was the point of visiting him if he didn't even know who they were? Shira was grabbing the socks out of his hand. He grabbed them back.

"Gently," his mother warned. "And I'm going to make today my late day, and we'll get into the kitchen and bake up some chocolate chip oatmeal cookies to fatten him up a little."

It was just about then that she took notice of Elisha's total lack of enthusiasm. But it wasn't about baking cookies. "Hello there . . ." she said. "This is such a nice idea, why do you look so miserable?"

Elisha tried to dispel some of his gloom as he responded, "I'm *not*. Just who else is going?"

"Well . . . Sammy Cohen, Michael Levy and you."

Elisha absorbed her words. Principal Oholiov knew real well about the seating arrangements in class. He didn't just pick three kids, he picked out three representatives, one Kohen, one Levite and one plain old someone from Israel, him. Probably hoping it would help bring back Professor Bezalel's memory.

OPTICAL ILLUSIONS 71

Shira started throwing the socks on the floor, and when Elisha put them back in the basket she became outraged and started having a tantrum. His mother ignored it.

"Well, anyway, *I'm* really pleased that Principal Oholiov picked you."

Elisha rolled his eyes. He really didn't mean to. It was almost an uncontrollable reflex, but it was enough, enough to get a whole five-minute lecture on being selfish. He looked down at the floor. Shira had worked herself into a baby monster at being ignored. She was beet red and thrashing around wildly all because of . . . a sock. His mother had to struggle to pick her up, but she still kissed her raging red colored head.

"I know, I know you're tired. Come on, sweetie. Let's get you into bed for a little nap."

Elisha sulked. Why was it that whenever Shira acted totally disgusting it was because she was 'tired'? She didn't look tired. He was really tired yesterday, and no one kissed his head. Maybe she just had a rotten personality. And what was she getting so tired about? Was it from having people running around the house doing things for her from morning until night . . . and just look at who had gotten the *selfish* lecture. And what was this bit about having to do this during summer vacation? It was like having to go back to school.

But it was even worse than that, because what really upset him was that his mother was right. One tiny opportunity to work on his selflessness had come up, to visit a sick teacher in the hospital, and it was the *last* thing he wanted to do. He knew that he had no choice about going, but he understood that somehow he had to *want* to go. He tried, but it was a leap, and he just couldn't do it.

Dr. Brody listened to the last audio file of his most entertaining, albeit entirely delusional patient.

Twenty two foundation letters. I permute them; I weigh them and transform them. I form substance out of chaos, and make the non-existent exist. My witnesses are the universe, year and soul. Their end is embedded in their beginning, and their beginning in their end. All of them oscillate cyclically and emerge through 231 Gates, and everything emanates from one Name.

Dr. Brody hit stop and then spoke into the mike attached to his laptop. "Jonathan Marks. 22 year old male. Arrived 25th June seeking hypnotherapy, claiming that four years prior his high school principal and teacher/mentor, one Professor Daniel Bezalel, 'erased' all his memories of the 'Chambers' program which he attended between the ages of 11 and 18, and which he describes as a clandestine summer school held in a subterranean vault under the Western Wall in the Old City of Jerusalem." Dr. Brody caught his breath and rubbed his eyes before he continued.

"Patient possesses above average intelligence, a photographic memory and an overactive imagination. He exhibits varying degrees of a fantasy prone personality, paranoid personality disorder, megalomania, introjection with said mentor and FMS. Patient will be referred to psychotherapy." Dr. Brody put down the microphone, took a bite of his croissant and mused. 'FMS'—'False Memory Syndrome'—in Jonathan's case should be renamed '*Fantasy* Memory Syndrome . . .'

Keren barely knocked and then walked straight into his office, humming and holding a brown manila enve-

OPTICAL ILLUSIONS 73

lope that sported a small collection of British stamps. She waved the envelope in the air and said, "I've got that piece of registered mail you wanted from Dr. Simmons at Cambridge."

"Yes, *wanted* as in past tense," he said sourly and then casually told her to leave it on his desk. When Jonathan Marks' case had still intrigued him, Dr. Brody had called in a favor to get his hands on *Sir* Professor Daniel Bezalel's 'revolutionary new physics theory' that was apparently too confidential to access online. He had hoped that it could shed some light on Jonathan's delusionary and obsessive behavior vis-à-vis his mentor. Once Keren was safely back at the reception desk, Dr. Brody immediately opened the envelope. Even though the case was thankfully closed in his mind, curiosity still called.

He was disappointed to see that there were no more than ten pages in the envelope, but then he noted that he was looking at some sort of confidential executive summary. He made himself a double espresso, reclined and read the first six pages. And he needed another double espresso after he finished reading it, because only another strong caffeine rush would enable him to digest what he had just perused. Whichever way you looked at it, it was utterly fascinating, and he was flabbergasted. He straightened the printed white papers in his hands and reread the document, trying to absorb the concepts.

Our thoughts travel at the speed of light. That was the introduction to Professor Bezalel's theory. Scientists were light-years away from figuring out how to travel *physically* at the speed of light, but our minds were already doing it. The professor had even formulated a method to measure the speed of thought. It was an incomprehensible sequence of numbers, symbols and letters which Dr. Brody skipped over. But it supposedly proved unequivocally that human thoughts could reach a speed of 186,282 miles per second. And that was only where the theory began . . . He then went on to make the outrageous claim that if we could access this *speed-of-light* electromagnetic energy in our brains, we could also harness enormous and unlimited *powers*. Dr. Brody breathed in deeply and looked out his window at the panoramic view. It was outlandish science fiction, yet it made sense in an outrageous sort of way.

The rest of the document went from ludicrous to preposterous in his opinion when Professor Bezalel started building on Einstein's famous space-time continuum to posit that there was actually a *fifth dimension* and it was located in *our own minds*. He claimed that 'consciousness' or 'soul' was a dimension which we were continuously interacting in, and we were 'moving' around in it just like we move through space and time, except with the potential to reach the *speed of light*. He also asserted that this 'fifth dimension' wasn't bound by space or time. Dr. Brody leaned back in his chair. It was all hauntingly familiar. He could recall Jonathan rambling on about some fifth dimension on more than one occasion. But, he had never given it much attention, because it was less bizarre than most of the other things that came out of his mouth during their hypnosis sessions. Dr. Brody also couldn't help feeling personally affronted; after all, psychiatrists certainly didn't need the theoretical physics gurus muscling in on their 'consciousness' territory.

The next part was where Dr. Brody was sure that the professor's rabbi persona came in, because he postulated that in the 'speed of light fifth dimension of consciousness' there was a different set of directions that a

OPTICAL ILLUSIONS 75

person's mind moved in. Unlike space where there was north-south/east-west/up-down, or time where you had minutes/hours/past-present-future, in the 'fifth dimension' the directions went from good to evil, right to wrong, truth to falsehood, etc.

Dr. Brody found that difficult to swallow. He got up from his chair and started to walk in a circle around his office.

I'm walking through three-dimensional space now. I can move up or down, right or left, he thought, *and I'm definitely moving through the fourth dimension of time, forward that is.* He looked at his watch and watched the seconds go by. *And yes, I'm thinking all of this as well. Could I possibly be moving around in this fifth dimension with my thoughts traveling at the speed of light?* Dr. Brody closed his eyes and tried another test. *Yes, I can easily conjure up images in my memory from the past and also imagine my life in the future. Does that mean that this supposed fifth dimension isn't bound by space or time?*

Dr. Brody sat down at his desk. *Could it be that my thoughts are moving in different directions on some moral compass? I suppose if I'm trying to help out a patient, then they are. But, what if I'm wondering how I can have superhuman powers by harnessing the speed-of-light energy in my mind?* Dr. Brody immediately dropped his train of thought. It was disconcerting, and he didn't want to have anything to do with it.

He took hold of the last page. It was the only one that he hadn't read up until now, and he expected it to just be a summary. But he was wrong.

Professor Bezalel *wasn't* just a theorist. He supported developing techniques to harness the speed-of-light energy in the human brain through a series of *experiments* which would be performed in various fields, and one of those fields was *altering consciousness!* He claimed that there were meditation techniques that involved right brain and left brain, 'verbal and non-verbal' consciousness, that could all be used to harness the speed-of-light energy and redirect it for empowerment—meaning that with the right training *everyone* could have super human powers! He even maintained that the 'ancients' were much more advanced with their meditation techniques for mind empowerment than modern man. He thought it highly unfortunate that most of these techniques were lost and recommended researching them more carefully, especially the ancient art of Kabbalah. He even made the incredible assertion that his own revolutionary theory was based on an ancient manuscript, called 'The Book of Creation,' that was the first to postulate a five and potentially ten-dimensional universe. And then Dr. Brody's hands started shaking uncontrollably . . . Professor Bezalel *believed* that these methods would be most effective on *children*—because their minds could be trained during the early formative and developmental stages of the brain, when it would be easiest for them to acquire the techniques needed for accessing the *speed-of-light* power in their brains—as easy as . . . learning a new language . . . .

Dr. Brody thought that he had washed his hands of Jonathan and his outlandish fantasy world. But how could he dismiss it all outright *now?* There was certainly evidence in his hands for major suspicion. Could it be that Jonathan's 'Chambers' were none other than one big laboratory experiment run by *Sir* Professor Bezalel? He *was* recommending all sorts of mind experimentation. Dr. Brody laid the paper neatly back on his desk. *A teacher experimenting on unsuspecting children?* If that

OPTICAL ILLUSIONS 77

was the case, he had indeed stumbled onto a situation with extreme repercussions. Maybe Jonathan *was* a victim after all!

The three boys sat in complete silence during the whole ride with Principal Oholiov as their chauffeur. It was clear that none of them felt privileged to be 'hand-picked' for this assignment. But they were luckily spared any mid-summer lecture by their principal, because he was on his cellphone the whole time. That made it easier for everyone's lackluster mood.

The usually active boys entered the hospital room awkwardly. Each of them was reserved and dutifully carrying home-made somethings in his bag. Principal Oholiov stood behind them, gently ushering them in with his arms stretched across all three of their backs and pushing them forward. He had the worst forced cheerfulness in his voice announcing their arrival.

"Now just have a look at what I found!" he said loudly.

The three boys silently nodded their 'hellos'. Elisha was reluctant to even look up. There was a part of him that didn't want Professor Bezalel to remember *anything* about him, especially that day in the classroom when Professor Bezalel had stared at him so weirdly right before collapsing. Elisha took a quick peek, and the scene *was* bad for other reasons. Elisha wouldn't have believed that Professor Bezalel could ever get skinnier. But he had. His face was like a skeleton's sunk beneath his jet black hair, and it was frightening. Principal Oholiov must have realized it, which is why he was trying to make up for it with such a fake happy voice. It was more than sad. It wasn't so much the hospital, or the weight loss, or seeing the giant lying in bed. It was the eyes. Elisha thought they seemed dead. No more fire. No more Professor Bezalel.

The ghostly-looking man on the hospital bed stared blankly at the boys, while Principal Oholiov led the conversation. "Now see if you can remember Sammy *Cohen,* Michael *Levy* and of course little Elisha *Davidson.*"

He was obviously accenting their last names, and Elisha could have done without the 'little' introduction part. The large skeleton with black hair nodded at them without the slightest interest. It all seemed so terrible to Elisha. Professor Bezalel of all people would have probably died just to have a talk with Elisha right now. And here it took all of Principal Oholiov's perseverance to keep up the uncomfortable one-way conversation.

It will be over soon, was the only comforting thought in Elisha's head. Conversation about the weather and the new plans for the school and how they were spending their summer vacations kept things running for a painful ten minutes more, but without even the slightest help or interest from Professor Bezalel himself. Principal Oholiov got the message.

"Okay Daniel, I think the boys have to go home now, but they'll come back again for another visit. Right, boys?" he added chirpily, motioning them to respond.

They all nodded obediently, and each said, "Goodbye, Professor Bezalel," in an unplanned chorus.

Whew, thought Elisha, *freedom.* It was just then that a tight boney hand shot out from nowhere and grabbed his arm with force. It was so unexpected. It was uncontrollable, but it happened. Elisha let out a short but very loud scream of fright. It took less than a fraction of a second for everyone to realize that it was only Professor

OPTICAL ILLUSIONS 79

Bezalel's hand that had quickly grabbed Elisha. But Sammy was already letting out a monstrous snort to repress his laugh, even though his hand was firmly clenched over his mouth. Michael was practically swallowing his whole fist, but choking laughter sounds were still coming out.

Principal Oholiov had quickly maneuvered both of them so that they were practically out the door. He used his loudest forced-pleasant booming voice to cover the snorts and chokes, calling out, "Daniel, is there something you wanted from Elisha?"

Now it was Principal Oholiov who was holding Elisha's arm and drawing him close to his side. For a minute it seemed like there was a flash of something. But Professor Bezalel's vacant eyes just looked at the ceiling.

"No. No. It's just that for a split second I thought there was something that I remembered about him." He studied Elisha hard again, almost pleading with his own memory. "No. It's gone." He looked at Elisha again. "No. No. Nothing familiar."

For Elisha the glint of recognition was even more horrifying than him grabbing his arm.

Principal Oholiov was of course furious about the whole fiasco. He sent a stabbing look at Elisha. That ridiculous girlish scream had certainly ruined that key moment that could have been a breakthrough for Daniel's memory. He gathered his car keys and the boys and curtly ushered them through the maze of hospital corridors. He was in his own thoughts as the boys walked ahead of him. He had never liked the Davidson kid. It wasn't that he didn't like Elisha personally, he just always disliked the 'pretty boy' type. He had enough experience to know how they always turned out in ten years. All the girls would fall in love with his looks, he'd break their hearts and become conceited and selfish in the process, and would surely find some very materialistic way to spend the rest of his life. That type was *never* good scholar material, and even worse Chambers material—*Jonathan Marks being the prototype*. And here he was acting all squeamish with that scream of his. You'd think a mouse had run past him. Quite honestly, the hand that jolted out had also caught him completely off guard, but letting out a horror movie scream was simply inexcusable! It completely ruined the only flash of recognition that Daniel had had since the accident.

As they rode down the elevator, Ezra realized that he would have to be sweet as sugar now to the boy, especially because he'd probably never want to come back after having practically leapt out of his skin. But there was no doubt the boy would *have* to come back, and fast. He might be a key to unlocking Daniel's memory, whether he wanted to or not. He'd manage to find a way of bringing the Davidson kid back. Principals always had ways of being *very* convincing. As for the other two clowns, he'd send them straight to detention for laughing. Except, he reminded himself, that they were in the middle of summer vacation, so he'd have to wait another month and a half. There weren't too many options. He would have to make do with a lecture in the car on the way home—the *whole* way home.

The four walked through the hospital parking lot without saying a word. Elisha was thrilled to be back in the normal fresh air. Hospitals were depressing places. He hated them. He couldn't wait to get out of there. He felt he had stretched his selflessness to the maximum for one day. And it was only too obvious that he'd have to spend the rest of his life living down the incident with

OPTICAL ILLUSIONS

his classmates. He'd be teased for eternity on this one. He was sure of it.

It was only when all three boys were securely fastened in the back seat that Principal Oholiov found his voice. The lecture started with the word 'selfish'. It was only a second, but Elisha also caught the pained expression on Principal Oholiov's face. Then he remembered just how personal it was: after all, the principal kept calling Professor Bezalel his brother-in-law.

The second lecture in one day about being selfish wasn't lost on Elisha. It was a wakeup call, and he knew it. Visiting Professor Bezalel could be the key for Elisha. It could be like taking a selflessness training course, which was what he needed most for the Ispaklaria. He wondered if that was being selfish? Sammy and Michael weren't saying a word, but the few side glances they made in his direction during the trip home always ended with more stifled giggles. But Elisha's mind was made up. When Principal Oholiov reached the closest drop-off point for his house, he respectfully turned to him.

"I'm sorry about what happened, Principal Oholiov. I didn't mean for it to happen, I really didn't . . . I just kind of got surprised. I, I could come back and visit Professor Bezalel if you think it would be good, you know, to try and make up for it."

All three of them were staring at him now and much to his amazement neither Sammy nor Michael were laughing. They even seemed to be looking at him with a sort of admiration. As for Principal Oholiov, he seemed to be in total shock. He was still in lecture mode, so it was hard to switch, but he did manage to speak.

"Well . . . that's very good of you, Elisha, and I am going to take you up on that. Have a good rest of the day."

Ezra Oholiov didn't drive off that quickly. He was watching Elisha through his rear view mirror making his way into the tiny streets of the Old City. *Well I'll be darned.* He was wrong about the boy. Dead wrong, and that was unusual for him. After all, he had 12 years of being a principal to guide his instincts. He laughed to himself. He still loved getting a good lesson.

The room wasn't circular and the walls weren't black and it wasn't underground. The room was very bright. It was lit with natural light and fake light. Someone was speaking to her. They were speaking fast and it was like being bombarded. A different voice was saying "Once upon a time . . ." She studied the three words and understood they were meaningless. You couldn't put the number one on top of time. She stared at the nothingness on the ceiling. She was happy that it didn't bother the big people to leave ceilings empty of things. It was the only place left in the room where she could stare at wisdom. They were speaking again. She closed her eyes to block them out. She wanted to see the things she understood. To watch all the little dots and static forming into beautiful pictures and then changing their shapes as fast as the speed of light. A small girl was forcing her hands to take something. She opened her eyes and looked down. It was a strange plaything with eyebrows that were very long and took up too much of an oversized head. Its neck was stretched out and it only had half a body. It did have a beautiful dress. She was sure that whoever had made it had felt so bad that they gave it a beautiful dress to cover it. She never had a dress that was beautiful like this one. The dress had a letter on it. Not a letter that she knew. It was two

OPTICAL ILLUSIONS 83

tunnels on the road standing sideways. She could see it even though she was looking at the back. She could see everything when she looked at the back of anything. She could see the sides. She could see the front. She could see the top like a bird and she could see the bottom like an ant. She could. If she had wanted to *see* something. Other people turned things around in their hands to look or they walked all the way around big things to look because they only learned to see with their eyes. She wondered if their eyes were also painted on their faces and even if they stay opened all the time and even if they were very big and even if they were the color of blue they would still see almost nothing of any thing.

If you wanted to SEE, you could see when your eyes were closed. Eyes could also SEE if they were open in pitch blackness. Didn't they know that all the pictures would disappear if they always kept their eyes open in the light? The voice in the room was bombarding her with more words. She ran away. She just had to close her eyes. She wanted to see even more beautiful pictures than her own. She wanted to see the pictures that were dancing and twirling in the dark behind the eyes of the Arranger of Letters, the Other, and even the *Yessod*.

She saw. She saw chaos in the dark. Chaos and more chaos and more chaos. She smiled to herself and almost started laughing and then stopped herself. She forgot that if she laughed they would also want to know why.

After apologizing for being two minutes late, Ezra threw his car keys onto his desk and said matter-of-factly, "Well, we just ran out of two more options today—*day* six and counting . . ."

Akiva rubbed the back of his neck. "Sorry, I really thought the kids' visit had a chance."

Ezra said, "Zippo," and then unlocked his briefcase and pulled out a small black and worn leather-bound notebook. He handled it with extreme caution as if it was a bomb that needed to be detonated. Devorah's eyes lit up.

"You found his diary!"

"Actually, my dear sister Rebecca did, and at the bottom of the family laundry pile."

"Did you show it to Professor Bezalel yet?"

"Of course. Unfortunately, it wasn't a trigger. I think he even thought we were crazy—wondered why we were flipping a blank notebook in front of his face. However, my practical sister also had the good sense to give it to me, hoping that we could find something in here that could help."

Devorah put out her hand to take it, but Akiva took it instead and handed it right back to Principal Oholiov.

"It's private!"

"Not under these circumstances," Ezra said as he handed it to Devorah again. "And don't worry, I'm sure there isn't a single 'dear diary' in there."

Without ceremony, Devorah did a quick flip through the blank pages. She looked up from the notebook. "Seriously? It's all advanced physics formulas." Akiva grabbed the notebook back and studied one of the blank pages.

"They're *encrypted* advanced physics formulas. *Professor Bezalel*-encrypted!"

Ezra drummed his fingers on the desk. "It's so frustrating not to be able to see the print on these pages."

Akiva nodded his head, and in seconds a neat scrawl appeared across the notebook's pages in ancient Hebrew. Ezra was proficient in reading the hieroglyphic-style al-

OPTICAL ILLUSIONS 85

phabet, but he also knew that the real text was *in between* the lines. In Chamber One, the first thing they taught their initiates was how to read and write, which actually consisted of deprogramming the kids from automatic linear reading and writing. Ezra focused between the lines, but all he saw was a dizzying array of symbols, letters, triangles and numbers along with mathematical functions. He closed the notebook and chewed the inside of his cheek. "But couldn't you maybe try to even decode just *one,* because if we got lucky maybe . . ." As Ezra heard his own voice trail off, he realized just how absurd the idea was. The formulas would go down to the grave. He quickly motioned to Akiva to blank out the pages again.

Akiva hesitated. "I think you should go through it more carefully first. Maybe there is something in there—"

"No. Believe me, I know how these things work out. It's Murphy's Law. The minute you make this legible, that will be the same day that it falls into the wrong hands."

Akiva stood up while blanking out the pages. "I'm joining Devorah in the Foundation Vault."

Ezra managed a hint of a smile. "Great, but, there's *another* option I want to discuss with both of you first."

Devorah and Akiva sat down somewhat reluctantly.

Ezra tapped his pen on the desk. *Time to let the tiger out of the cage.* He breathed in deeply. "Your former classmate . . . ex-prodigy, expelled Chamber Seven Graduate, persona non grata, Jonathan Marks, a.k.a 'The Other'"—

Before Ezra finished speaking, Akiva had swiped the morning paper off the desk. "What nasty article did he write about us this time?"

Ezra shook his head and took the newspaper out of Akiva's hands. "I wish. It's worse than that. He's somehow regaining his Chambers training."

Akiva immediately stiffened and Devorah's whole body tensed.

"He paid Professor Bezalel a little hospital visit and gave him a message to pass on to me. Basically that he would restore Professor Bezalel's memory if we restored his."

Devorah crossed her arms tightly to hide their shaking: "But, that's impossible."

"Is it? I mean, which one is impossible? Is it impossible for one of you to restore Jonathan's memory? Or is it impossible that he could restore Professor Bezalel's?"

"They're both impossible!" Akiva said adamantly, "and why would you even think that *he* could do something we couldn't?"

Devorah stood up. "Stop! I *meant* that it's impossible for Jonathan to even remember that he *has* a fifth dimensional self! *Isn't it?*"

Ezra leaned back in his chair. "Since we're all still clueless as to *who* or *what* erased Jonathan's Chambers memories to begin with, we can't rule out that he's somehow back in the picture."

Akiva faced Devorah straight on. "Come on. Connect the dots. Everything makes sense now. Maybe you just don't want to admit that your high-school crush is behind this somehow?"

Devorah did her best to fight back a surge of anger. She didn't like how Akiva had grabbed the notebook right out of her hands before, but *now* he had just plummeted in her mind from a Seven to a Two. Maybe these were both red alerts that she should be paying more attention to . . . .

Ezra raised his hand. "Honestly. I didn't even want to consider it, but at this point, let's just be practical. Re-

OPTICAL ILLUSIONS

store Jonathan's memory and then he'll restore Professor Bezalel's, and we'll *somehow, God only knows how,* figure out how to deal with him afterwards."

Akiva started shaking his head. "*What!?* That would be tantamount to restoring all of his empowerment. Do you seriously want to take the risk . . ."

Ezra finished the thought in his mind . . . *of unleashing a Chamber Seven graduate attached to the dark side?*

Akiva jumped out of his chair. "He's the antithesis of everything that Professor Bezalel—that *we've all* been trying to achieve. Sorry. But he's a self-centered megalomaniac. If you empower *that*, the next thing he's going to do is . . . hmmm . . . let's see, how about taking over the world, for starters!"

Devorah jumped in, "Oh please!"

Ezra was still nodding away at Akiva when Devorah blurted out. "*Reality-check time!* I think it's pretty obvious that we don't have *any idea* how to restore memories, *period!*"

"Devorah, *I know* that Professor Bezalel personally trained you in selective memory erasure."

"Correct. The *Standard Foundation Vault Protocol* for Selective Memory Erasure, so?"

"So, you must also know how to reverse it."

"It's *irreversible,* and it was only for emergencies like a *tohu v'bohu* crisis. And I never even had one of those . . . And I do hope you know that it's a form of *karet.* It shouldn't even be in our hands—"

"It's ONLY *karet* for a Seven, and he's *not* one!"

Devorah's ringtone interrupted the conversation. 'Unknown caller' appeared on the screen. Devorah tried to sound calm when she said, "Speaking of 'The Other.'"

Ezra motioned her quickly to answer it.

Devorah touched 'speaker' and laid the phone on Principal Oholiov's desk. She noticed that Akiva's jaw was tightly clenched.

Jonathan's voice rang out clearly. "I'm surprised. I hope it wasn't just for the satisfaction of hanging up on me."

Devorah coolly responded, "What?"

"I've got a problem."

"Really? Only one?"

"Devorah. Please. If I'm calling you it's because I have nowhere else to turn."

Devorah's muscles tensed. *The master of manipulation.*

"It's a Chamber Five problem."

Ezra, Devorah and Akiva all exchanged meaningful looks. Jonathan was clearly up to Chamber Five. It was a moment of relief. At least he wasn't a Six.

Devorah stayed silent.

"You owe me a Five, Devorah. You know that."

Devorah hung up.

Akiva was flustered. "What's that 'you owe me' bit!"

"Look. You weren't there when Simon Zoma turned my hair into a pile of tarantulas. Jonathan was our Chamber Five recess guard, and thankfully he was."

Akiva immediately backed down.

Ezra suddenly tried to suppress a huge smile. "*What if* he's in *tohu v'bohu*? That would be too good to be true . . ."

"If he's only up to Five, that would also mean that, as usual, he's lying through his teeth. He can't do a thing for Professor Bezalel."

Devorah put her emotions into check and turned thoughtful. "And as usual, he has an ulterior motive . . ."

She stared at her phone. "If it was me . . . and I was on my way back . . . the one single thing I'd want would be to gain access to the Foundation Vault. I wouldn't be surprised if he pretends to be in *tohu v'bohu* just so that we take him in."

"Meet with him. We absolutely need to find out where he's holding."

"And then what?"

"I don't care if he's in *tohu v'bohu* or he just needs you to clean up some monstrous mess he created. He needs to be cut off *now*."

Devorah glared at Principal Oholiov and then turned to Akiva for support.

He looked her steadily in the eyes and quoted an ancient adage. "If you're compassionate to the cruel, you'll ultimately become cruel to those deserving compassion."

Ezra nodded. "Lure him into the Foundation Vault and then perform your *Standard Foundation Vault Protocol!*" Ezra massaged his neck and then added, "Professor Bezalel would have wanted you to."

Devorah closed her eyes. It was better than looking at the two threatened egos in front of her, and it gave her a moment to contemplate yet another mystery of the universe. How were *men* ever able to let go of their egos long enough to achieve the lowest level of selflessness? And yet she knew that the truly greats throughout history had miraculously done just that, against all innate odds, and especially Professor Bezalel . . . *and no, he wouldn't! He would have laid down his life to save Jonathan.*

It was wrap-up time, and Jessie was feeling satisfied about himself because Aaron had actually turned out to be a good choice and not just a charitable one. It was only one day, but he had already worked three times faster than anyone they ever had before, on top of being a virtual Samson in strength. He even repositioned all the bookcases with a smile when Menashe found a major shelving error, and the biggest surprise was that he was actually bright. He managed to understand Menashe's complex cataloguing system after only one explanation. None of the other hired hands had ever looked past the boxes they were carrying. But Jessie still wasn't entirely at ease, especially now that he had deciphered *all* the symbols that Aaron had brought him. He was still trying to wrap his mind around it, because he had never seen the combination before—ancient star script alphabet with advanced physics formulas. In a sense they were both obscure languages, just on opposite ends of time/history. Obviously, *someone* who was familiar with both had written the strange text of symbols, and that in itself seemed like an impossibility.

Jessie stared at the five equations that were under the heading 'Fifth Dimension'. They were meaningless to his eye, but he already had the top brains at both the Weizmann Institute and the Technion trying to crack the physics formulas. So far, all they could tell him was that one of the equations was remotely similar to Professor Daniel Bezalel's fifth dimension work, emphasis on *remotely*. Jessie wondered . . . maybe, the formulas were fictitious? Or maybe the top brains in the country were slacking? They still hadn't come up with any explanations for the selective sonic boom phenomenon either. Jessie checked Aaron's bio again. It was clean as a whistle, and his periodic stays in the psychiatric hospital seemed totally understandable considering what the man had

OPTICAL ILLUSIONS   91

gone through. But why was he spending so much time with Elisha? Didn't an adult have better things to do? Jessie squelched that theory too. It was only logical that a man who had lost two sons would gravitate to that sort of thing. Tamar was surely right that Elisha was filling the role of a surrogate son. Jessie stopped and cleaned his glasses. All these strays that his wife liked to pick up were more than annoying. As far as Jessie was concerned they were security risks, each and every one of them, even Gila, Shira's 15 year old babysitter—okay, maybe that was an exaggeration. But he really *wished* she would just stick with the non-risk categories like the autistic kids or animals. He smiled. His allergy to cats and dogs had precluded the latter, and thankfully so, or their home would be a Noah's ark animal shelter by now. That reminded him—he'd better get the name of a child psychiatrist. He quickly closed the document he was looking at when he heard Menashe ascending the stairs to his office terrace.

"Ah, the air of Olympus," Menashe said as he arrived at the landing of the spiral staircase slightly out of breath.

Jessie always hated interruptions, and he didn't look up from his work. In any case, his staff was used to talking to his back.

"How long do we have Aaron for?" Menashe inquired seriously.

Jessie answered still facing his screen, "As long as Hades needs him."

Menashe said, "Great!" and was already descending the steps when he called up, "but, like I told you, it's also a waste of a great mind down there."

Jessie said, "Aren't you all . . ." Then he stopped and leaned over the banister and asked, "How great?"

Menashe looked straight up and said, "He's really

up there!"

Jessie practically shouted downward, "The man barely finished high school."

Menashe stopped and held the railing. "I know, I'm not talking Mensa member, but he's just got a very good head on his shoulders." He looked down for a minute and then looked back up. "Or maybe it just seems like that because you usually give us the brain dead ones."

Jessie rolled his eyes to himself. Okay, it was true, on his wife's request he had filled their temporary moving jobs on more than one occasion with what she called 'highly-functioning mentally challenged individuals,' but at least it was clear that Aaron wasn't the author of the symbol text. So where *did* he get it from?

Unavoidable. That's all that came to Dr. Brody's mind. It was simply unavoidable. If he was going to get to the bottom of the Jonathan Marks case, he would have to invest some non-billable hours to do some background research, and probably outside the confines of his office. The Internet was glutted with so many outlandish and bizarre Kabbalah references that he might as well have been searching for UFOs. Dr. Brody sighed as he realized that he would have no other choice but to try and find a legitimate and non-virtual source offline. It irked him that his many degrees left him ill-equipped to deal with the subject and feeling grossly inadequate. He was *far* from being a spiritual man, and having been the recipient of an anti-religious upbringing, he could proudly say that he was a man of science in every respect; which was why he was now in the unenviable position of having to find a Doctor of Theology, or namely a rabbi. Finding one

OPTICAL ILLUSIONS

wouldn't be difficult, and in his opinion there were far too many to be found, but his instincts told him that not just any rabbi would do. He'd have to find one of those authentic Kabbalah gurus. His mouth grimaced with the distaste of it all. He asked Keren to handle the research. It turned out that she couldn't have been more thrilled and even knew exactly which Doctor of Theology to send him to.

CHAPTER FIVE

Full of yourself

A TIME TO DISCARD

"Where's my bag?" Tamar Davidson called out as she felt behind the sofa.

Jessie didn't hear her because he was calling out from the kitchen, "Hey, what happened to my coffee thermos?" Ten seconds later it turned into. "Someone took my phone!"

Aaron pretended to be oblivious to the morning hubbub until it pulled itself together. Jessie was the first one out the door without any missing pieces. Now Tamar was searching Shira's baby bag, making a mental check list . . . diapers, bottle, formula, change of clothes, pacifier. "Wait . . . where's the wipes?" She patted the bag's outer zipped pocket and then handed it to Gila while giving Shira a big hug. She acknowledged Aaron with a flustered "I'm telling you this house is the Bermuda Triangle."

Aaron smiled.

Tamar looked nervously at her watch. "I'm going to be ten minutes late *again*." She called out to Gila, "There's lunch in the fridge." *If that hasn't disappeared* . . . and then she turned to Aaron. "Oh. Would you mind waking

FULL OF YOURSELF 95

up Elisha before you go out to work? I know it's summer vacation, but I just don't want him to get too used to sleeping late all the time."

Aaron answered with a "No problem" as Tamar Davidson rushed out the door, and then he proceeded directly to Elisha's room an hour and half earlier than requested. He loudly entered the room and said, "Your Mom wants you to get up."

Elisha was thrilled and was washed and dressed in minutes.

Aaron was transferring the Ispaklaria key from one hand to the other while saying, "I think this has gotta be our new schedule. The way I figure it, we've got a safe one-hour window between your Mom gettin' off to work and me goin' to work. So, you can kiss your lazy summer mornin's goodbye."

That was fine with Elisha, and he could barely wait as Aaron fiddled around with the Ispaklaria key and kept squinting his eyes like he was aiming a gun or something. But there wasn't a single angle or position that worked. Aaron kept talking to the triangle with increased frustration. Threats didn't work either, and after a full hour's worth of failure they both gave up. Aaron seemed so disgusted when he left for work that Elisha was worried he might not want to bother with it again. Elisha was even convinced that the key must have broken. He would have moped on that for a while, except that five minutes later Josh was at his front door with a soccer ball in his hand.

"Hey, what are you doing here?" Elisha asked. "Aren't you in soccer camp?"

"Yup, I am, and meet the new captain of the team."

"Really?"

"Yup, but today I'm off 'cause there's a day trip to

the zoo and I got myself out of it."

Elisha couldn't help feeling a sting of jealousy. He remembered how his father had laughed when he asked to go to soccer camp after the Chambers were cancelled. He had said it was "an exorbitant waste of time and money."

"We've got the most amazing coach," Josh bragged, "and he's showed us moves like you wouldn't believe."

"Really?"

"Come on, let's go to the park and I'll show you."

It was awesome, and it wasn't. In just two weeks of training, Josh had turned into a much better player than Elisha, and he had *never* been better than him. He even wiped him out. Elisha couldn't hide his aggravation at being defeated. He could just see himself if he was there—he'd be the captain instead of Josh. On the walk home, Josh couldn't stop talking about his new prowess.

"I can't believe it. *I* killed *you*! That's like never happened before!"

Elisha just wanted to get rid of him, but apparently he had rescheduled his zoo day to stick around the whole time. He followed Elisha straight into his house and then into his room.

"Did you see? I mean, I *really* got good!"

All Elisha wanted to do was to change the subject already. Maybe in the confines of his room things would be different. After all, what was snotty soccer camp compared to the Ispaklaria? It even out-ranked the world cup. No, it would even outrank a trillion million universe cups if there were any.

"Hey, you moved it. Why do you still keep this old thing in your room?" Josh asked with his nose scrunched up.

Elisha was suddenly considering showing off the *real*

FULL OF YOURSELF 97

Ispaklaria. Josh *was* his best friend. He was about to go for it until he noticed Josh's reflection, and one look was enough to change his mind. "I don't know. I just like it." Elisha answered as he watched Josh's reflection intently. It was a really scary, dark-looking black shadow, so thick and blobby that it seemed to stick out of the stone. *What's with that?*

Josh got closer and started touching the stone's surface on all sides, and then Elisha thought he had it figured out. It was because Josh was so *full of himself* that his reflection was solid as a black rock.

"But what's it even do?" Josh asked as he started bouncing the soccer ball against it.

Elisha shrugged, "Oh nothing, really," but he had to hold himself back from grabbing the ball out of Josh's hands. How dare he bounce a stupid ball against an Ispaklaria! Shira suddenly scampered into his room at a fast pace. She was screeching, crawling and giggling. She pulled herself to a standing position using the stone and then started wiping her gooked-up cookie and saliva hands all over it, leaving thick smear marks. *Her* reflection was regular, so he hadn't mistaken Josh's. Elisha shouted at her, "*Stop!*" and started pulling her away when Gila barged right into the room. Elisha immediately snapped at her.

"You could knock, you know?"

Gila twisted her mouth into a nasty growl. "Really, why would I do that? I didn't see Shira knocking and I'm much more important." She bent down to pick up Shira, who was gooping up the mirror stone even more, and said, "Shira's trying to clean your dirty rock. Isn't that sweet!" She laughed and then broke out in an annoying song. "This is the way we wash the mirror, wash the mirror, wash the mirror. This is the way we wash the mirror, early in the morning."

The song was more than enough to enrage Elisha, but he was so taken aback by Gila's reflection that he couldn't think up even one good mean thing to say back to her. He stared at her reflection in horror. It was a dark blood-red color and was spreading out further than where her own reflection should be. Her singing voice suddenly turned into an echo that sounded like loud screaming in his mind. Elisha shook his head, but it kept getting louder and shriller. He couldn't stand the screaming sound of her voice for a second more. It sounded like someone was being murdered. She was turning his mirror stone into that pool of blood again. It was *her*. Elisha's ears were throbbing with the screams, and he had to shout out in full volume over the loud sounds in his head. He didn't even realize just how loud he had to shout!

"GET OUT OF MY ROOM THIS SECOND OR I'LL KILL YOU!"

Gila's real face was now turning as dark red as her shadow. She put both her hands on her hips and grabbed Shira and slammed the door closed.

"Whoa," said Josh with a completely shocked face, and he made a fast exit too.

Elisha was left alone staring at the Ispaklaria and shaking. He felt sick. Why had he shouted like a madman? It *felt* wrong, and he felt strangely scared of himself. But it wasn't him. *It's them!! It's not my fault that there are evil black and red shadowy people running around my room!* He thought about 'full-of-himself' Josh, and his mood worsened just as he heard, "Hey Kiddo."

Aaron was back. He was opening a box of cereal and seemed in too good a mood to Elisha. "You've got

FULL OF YOURSELF   99

me for a *whole hour.* The lights went off in the dungeon
and Menashe let me off." He rubbed his hands together
excitedly and motioned toward the stone. "We're gonna
to try again, because now I've got a new *plan.*"

Elisha guiltily glanced at the Ispaklaria. As usual,
Aaron still didn't have any reflection whatsoever. Rav
Kadosh had told him it was because Aaron was one of the
36 and because he was so selfless he didn't even reflect,
but Elisha wasn't allowed to ever divulge that to Aaron.
Well, at least he was still *normal.* He continued listening
to Aaron without even looking up at him.

"You see. I've realized that our whole problem is just
that we're disorganized. You should see this guy Menashe
down in the archives, he's kind of a maniac, but he's
got everythin' catalogued, color-coded, cross-referenced,
key-worded, and I think memorized on top of it all. And
he's always sayin' 'there's a method to my madness.' That's
what we've gotta do."

Elisha looked blankly at Aaron.

"We need to be methodical. We need to keep a record
of every failure, the time, what we tried, what worked,
what didn't. It's called trial and error and it's the only
way we'll figure out what the real right way is to use this
key with the Ispaklaria."

Elisha didn't even want to look at him again. Didn't
Aaron remember that *selflessness* was the key? Elisha *had.*
Did Aaron have some kind of method for *that?* Elisha
was still clueless, but he had a pretty good feeling that
he had blown it completely today.

"And you especially, you've *really* got to get organized," Aaron said while searching for a notebook.

Elisha had no idea what he was suggesting.

"You've got to write down a list of questions to ask

King Solomon. 'Cause last time you didn't even open up your mouth, right? And then when he answers them, you've got to write it all down and keep it in a diary. That way you don't get all confused, and then we just might figure out what we've got on our hands here." Aaron handed him a pen and paper and said, "Start writin' out our list of questions."

Aaron's mood was infectious, and Elisha was practically leaping out of his skin to see King Solomon again *and* to get answers. He was already at question twelve when Aaron stopped him.

"Okay, now we'll go for it," he said, but first sent Elisha off for a pack of baby wipes to clean up the Ispaklaria. He then checked his watch and wrote the time down on a piece of paper. He pointed the Ispaklaria key directly into the middle of the stone and wrote that down too. He went through his new maddening method of times, angles and various positions, but there were no water*ups* even at logged entry #13. But Aaron was relentless.

"Here, let's try something else. Maybe if both of us go into the field of vision at once." Aaron awkwardly held the Ispaklaria key over his own head while pushing Elisha full force with his arm.

Elisha suddenly felt a mild pulling sensation surrounding his body, like he was being gently swallowed, and before he even had a chance to brace himself, his room took on the distorted reflections of a fun house mirror. He found himself looking directly into the King's meditation chamber, *except* that only half of him was there. His body felt stuck right in the middle of the stone, and he couldn't get out. And the half that was there, was see-through like a ghost. Elisha could see King Solomon at the far end on his magnificent throne. He once again

FULL OF YOURSELF

felt totally overwhelmed at seeing the great man, but King Solomon wasn't alone this time. There were two guards at his side and they looked like mammoth towering gladiators. One of them spoke.

"Now you may behold with your own eyes that I spoke the truth. By my life, he is a demon, half in this world and half in the other."

The other guard nodded, "Yes, demons are always small, are they not?"

The first guard, reached for his sword, but King Solomon held up his hand and dismissed them both. He called out to Elisha from the throne.

"Well, my young descendant, what took you *so* long?"

That was one of the questions Elisha had on his list. Why *wasn't* the Ispaklaria thing working? It was broken or something and now he was even stuck solid and couldn't budge!

King Solomon arose from his throne. "Hmmm . . . Yes. I can see why. I shall tell you why you are only half here. Given the state of your selflessness today, it is *only* on the merits of the *Kohen Gadol* that you are receiving and not on your own. And indeed one does get quite stuck when one is too full of one's self."

Elisha felt like disappearing, and in any case it seemed half of him had. The King walked toward him.

"Even though you are at a tender age, you *can* acquire selflessness. Indeed, you *will have to*. For that is the key to your problem, or should I say the technical problem you are experiencing with your key."

The King pointed his finger in Elisha's direction and then traced the outline of his body in the air. The next second Elisha disconnected and fell forward. He turned around half expecting to see half his body still stuck in the wall, but instead there was just a faint mark, outlining where his body had been, right in the middle of the distinct shadowy rectangular shape of his mirror stone. Well, at least moving the stone to the east side of his room had worked. He could come right to the King from now on, *IF* he was selfless enough.

King Solomon said, "Shall we?"

Elisha was nodding his head, but then caught sight of his arms. He was still translucent like a ghost. King Solomon waved it off.

"Do not be troubled. Believe me, most people are really never all there. And in fact there are those moments in life where such a state is even entirely desirable."

Elisha suddenly felt his back being pushed and a tinny echoing voice saying, "Can ya at least try and help?" Elisha shook his head. He was still in the King's chambers, and he tried concentrating his attention back onto the King. He was about to get up the courage to ask his first question, when King Solomon preempted him.

"As for your twelve questions, let it be known that with each vision of ultimate reality you will receive special gifts of understanding. These are the true gifts of time from the Timeless One. And in *time*, you will understand. Now behold! I will record everything I am about to reveal to you."

The aquamarine room started to sparkle brilliantly in every direction. It was disorienting and made it hard, really hard to concentrate. Then Elisha felt a tap on his shoulder. It was Aaron's tin-man voice saying, "Good, we got one arm in there. Hey, why is it back out again?"

The King wasn't waiting for him to pay attention. He started speaking in his melodic voice, and as he spoke his words were forming into silvery rainbow strands throughout the room.

"Everything has its season, and there is a time for everything . . . Thus, my command is that you may *only* use the fourth dimension of time on the Ispaklaria key until I shall instruct you otherwise." The King opened his hand and a large Ispaklaria key appeared. He gently moved his hand in upward motion, and the key became suspended in midair while it grew to fill up half the chamber. "You will note that there are four time continuums in the fourth dimension of time."

Elisha could now clearly see each one, but he also felt Aaron smacking his head forward.

"The 'First Temple' field of vision is the ultimate reality of my illusion of time only, *except* on the 9th of Av. And then time will be locked at only *one* point. It will eternally be the dark time, and *always* at night. It is a point in time that is 385 years in the future from my time, in the illusion of time. *Never* try to access it yourself. Only upon my command shall you enter the 9th of Av."

Elisha was trying to figure what was going to happen in 385 years that was so *dark;* but the rainbow threads of words seemed like a meshy glimmering screen spinning around his head, and Elisha momentarily lost his balance from the dizzying lights. But King Solomon kept making more.

"The dark time is the point of THE destruction of the very Temple I was entrusted to build. Yet this one day of the year will only and *always* will be your goal. For on the *darkest* day of the year, there is a window of the *greatest* light."

Elisha felt panic stricken. He didn't have anything to write with. How was he supposed to record all the important information, especially with all the silvery words whirling around the room? Was the date 583 years away or was it 835? And now the annoying voice of Aaron was back in his head. It sounded like he was talking under water.

"*bl*—One more—*blup* time and we've got it."

The next second his awareness was back in the King's chambers.

"As for the other space-time continuums that the *Yessod* can receive, 'The Second Temple' spans 410 years, although I must say that it never was as fine as the First." The King's expression turned somber as he pointed again to the suspended Ispaklaria key. "The third illusion—'5766-5777'—is the Hebrew calendar years for *your* present lifeline to date, Elisha, son of David, son of Jessie. But it is the most *dangerous* illusion of time to tamper with. If there ever is a face to face meeting of your two selves at different ages, you will destroy both, and your energy will merge with the Timeless Reality. So, do not attempt it, unless it is worth dying for."

Elisha had really wanted to pay attention. He realized that everything being said was of utmost importance. But the half of him that was there apparently didn't include his brain. The King was now turning the key so that Elisha could clearly see the last symbol.

"The Eighth Kingdom of course is the world as we know it."

But Elisha had given up on focusing. He lost himself in the beautiful sight of the silvery rainbow threads reflecting on all sides of the shiny blue room, until he felt Aaron tugging at his shoulder and heard his voice echoing like it was in a cave.

"Forget, *forget* it *it it*. It's *it's it's* just *just just* not

FULL OF YOURSELF 105

not workin' *workin'*!"

Elisha shook his head and found his voice. If he didn't ask one question, Aaron would kill him. He couldn't remember a single one from his list, but now a new one had entered his mind.

"Your Majesty, what is the Eighth Kingdom?"

"Are you asking what is the world as we know it?"

There was shock in the King's voice even though his face was entirely calm. Elisha almost cringed. His first question was apparently a really stupid one. The King immediately put his hand on Elisha's ghostly shoulder.

"I am sorry . . . it is through no fault of your own . . . although I must say that the educational system *has* truly deteriorated beyond even my worse suppositions. My dear descendant, we *all* live in the Eighth Kingdom. The Eighth Kingdom started with Adam and Eve, of course, and is continuing to evolve until today, as in *your* present day, the year 5777."

Elisha said sheepishly, "Oh, sorry, I just didn't realize it was called the Eighth Kingdom that's all."

"Well, surely you know that there were seven kingdoms before?"

Elisha stayed quiet.

"Certainly you've seen the endless discoveries by paleontologists of Tyrannosaurus, Ceratosaurus, Stegosaurus . . ."

Elisha felt his mind had turned into mush at hearing the four unidentifiable words in a row.

King Solomon stopped himself and said, "Pardon me; I should have said dinosaurs to make it all perfectly clear. The previous seven kingdoms were quite different worlds, and *thankfully* all were destroyed before ours, the Eighth Kingdom."

Elisha's scattered brain was trying to absorb what he had just heard. He couldn't help wondering: did that mean that if he used the point of the 'Eighth Kingdom' on the Ispaklaria key, he could be *anywhere in the world* 'as we know it' *at any time?* Elisha knew he hadn't asked the question, but King Solomon still answered it.

"No. That would be level twelve, and I am afraid you have not even mastered level one yet." King Solomon pointed to the enlarged key again and said, "The fifth is the greatest and most powerful dimension of nothingness there is, and the fifth will take all your *time* and patience until *you* will be able to reveal it."

Elisha waited for more, but the King just said, "And now is *not* the time."

There was a tiny beep from Elisha's watch. It was the 13 minute mark that meant he only had five minutes left. This whole visit was a disaster, Elisha was sure of it. All the important stuff had come up, and he wouldn't remember a word, and Aaron had just said they were supposed to get organized and take notes. The room was now so packed full of silvery rainbow threads of words that Elisha was lightheaded just looking at them. His watch was beeping louder. With a wave of his hand the King was vacuuming the words from the room. They were being sucked with a twirling force into the King's outspread hand. The spinning was forming a rainbow silvery round shape that was vaguely familiar. If it wasn't for the strange setting, Elisha would have immediately realized that he had just been given a CD.

King Solomon put it into his ghostly hand and said, "Quite an unreliable way to store information; however, compatibility is what counts in our case. You are now in possession of a beginner's 'Instruction Manual for the

FULL OF YOURSELF 107

Ispaklaria Key: Chapter One, Timelessness.'"

Elisha couldn't hide the shock on his face, and the King added:

"Did I not say I will *record* everything I will reveal to you? Do you think perchance I would take the risk of you remembering only half of what I said?"

Suddenly, a loud voice rang out from the back of the massive hall.

"It is I, Benaiah son of Jehoiada, with an urgent message from Hiram, King of Tyre for His Majesty."

"Entry granted."

Elisha watched curiously as one of the power-ful-looking guards he had seen before handed a scroll to the King, along with a colorful parrot, and was dismissed. It was unmistakable. Elisha saw it. The Benaiah guy had a black shadow reflection on King Solomon's wall, just like Josh's. Elisha desperately blurted out another question that wasn't on his list.

"King Solomon, what is the meaning of people's reflections on the Ispaklaria stone?"

King Solomon's eyes lit up. "Oh, but I thought you found that definition in your Google Babel search. Did it not reveal to you that the Ispaklaria reflects the hearts and souls of men?"

Elisha nodded. That had been *one* of the definitions for Ispaklaria when he had searched for it online with Aaron. "But the colors, I don't know how to read the colors." Elisha started kicking his foot; it felt like Aaron was grabbing it.

"Ah yes! The color coding is my special enchantment for easy reference. You see, a king needs to be a keen judge of character. And . . . the *Yessod* will have to be an even *keener* one in order to be the *One Who Connects*."

King Solomon made a black shadow appear on the crystalline wall right near Elisha and said, "Those with a black shadow are my most loyal warriors. They are men that are willing to fight to the end and even die for what they believe in. They are very, very rare, and when I find one, I make those black shadow men the fearless and valiant leaders of my troops." King Solomon waved his hand and the shadow turned red. "Unfortunately, in your days red is a most common color. Although with your social standing, you may have only been exposed to their souls on what I believe you erroneously call 'reality shows.' It reveals those hearts and souls whose spirit is broken. I never allow red-shadowed people to leave my presence without giving them my help, *even* if I have just passed judgment *against* them in the royal court and even if they are *not* deserving. Their situation is too desperate and dangerous, and they often take their own lives." King Solomon focused his eyes on Elisha's ghostly body. "With the current state of your selflessness, *you,* my dear descendant are more in need of a red-shadowed person than they are in need of *you.* Or we may even be seeing less of one another than we are now . . ."

Elisha's watch let out a shrill beep, but he understood exactly what the King meant.

The King motioned Elisha to the shadow outlined on the wall and calmly added, "It is my sincere hope that you shall never encounter the color blue or yellow in your chambers."

Elisha tried to walk his ghostly body back into the stone's reverse shadow, but it was hard as a rock. He turned back to the King, who was already unfurling the scroll message. The King didn't look up but motioned him to carry on and said:

FULL OF YOURSELF   109

"In addition, do not be surprised if you temporarily acquire some of my gifts of wisdom on the same day of your visit. You might find yourself leaving with a bit more than you came with."

Elisha was doing his absolute best to remember that one, because if he could coordinate it with an end-of-year math test sometime, it could be very helpful. He took a deep breath and pressed his whole body as hard as he could against the rock-hard surface. He could feel that he was moving ever so slightly, but it was like he was a congealed fossil in a mass of solid stone. He tightened all his muscles and kept pushing forward slowly. His body felt like it was already fused into the rock, and it was a huge effort to get un-encrusted. Maybe he'd be stuck forever and they'd only find his body in the Ninth Kingdom. He breathed in deeply and relentlessly, willing himself forward. It took until he was almost blue in the face, but he finally made it out. And once he did, he never remembered feeling so lightweight and free. But the best part was being whole again.

For a moment, Elisha's room still looked like a two-dimensional reflection. He could see Aaron, who was totally focused on searching the bottom of his cereal box. The room started to slowly lose its flatness, and Elisha immediately asked in an annoyed voice: "Aren't you supposed to be guarding me or something?"

Aaron immediately tossed a handful of cereal crumbs into his mouth. "What are you talkin' about? I was watchin' your back side the whole time and tryin' to push you through." He shook his head. "Just forget it—it's just not workin' and it weirds me out."

"I know what went wrong. It's because I was kind of only half there." Elisha then handed Aaron the CD and said matter-of-factly, "Ispaklaria key instruction manual."

Aaron said, "Come off it." But he hovered anxiously right on top of Elisha like a bear while Elisha put the disc into his computer drive.

Elisha opened the file, and a document that looked like a parchment inscribed with black Hebrew letters appeared on the screen. Aaron pushed him to the side and cracked his knuckles.

"Leave this to me. I'm great with instruction manuals."

Aaron and Elisha quickly read the Hebrew writing. It was very straightforward, and Elisha vaguely remembered half of it, but the writing was disappearing at the speed they were reading it.

Aaron got up and seemed upset. He started pacing the room and said, "*That's it?*"

Elisha became disgruntled. "Why, it's a lot!"

Aaron wasn't satisfied. "It's somethin', OK, but it's still almost nothin'. We only got *one* side of the triangle key here. And since when is 'the world as we know it' called the 'Eighth Kingdom'?" Aaron was already searching online. Elisha looked curiously over his shoulder, but all that came up were B science fiction movies.

Aaron said, "You see, it doesn't exist!"

"You mean you didn't know that either?"

"Know what?"

"Oh good, I thought it was me. The King said there were seven worlds before ours. The ones with the dinosaurs and everything, well that was before . . . it must have been in the seven kingdoms before . . ."

Aaron scrunched up his face. "*What?!* What in the world are you talkin' about?" But he stopped himself and just breathed noisily through his nose and said, "Fine,

FULL OF YOURSELF 111

and what about that last side of the triangle? You know, that one with five strings of symbols that your dad is *still* trying to crack. There's not a *thing* in there about those."

Elisha tried to remember.

"The King did say something about the fifth dimension . . . something like we can't deal with it right now or something."

Aaron looked at Elisha sourly. "See what I meant about bein' organized? 'Cause we still didn't even get the most important answer, like *why in the world is any of this happenin'!!!!*"

Elisha was quick to respond, "But that *is* in there."

Aaron gave him a confused look. "Yeah? Where?"

"It said the 9th of Av is our goal!"

"Right. For *WHAT?*"

Elisha didn't have a clue, but then remembered. "But it said, didn't it say that we'll understand in *time?*"

Aaron squinted his eyes and then looked at his watch with annoyance. "Well, it's also *time* for me to get back to the dungeon. I'm sure by now the lights are back on in the Eighth Kingdom." He crunched up the cereal box, saying, "And can you at *least* try and do somethin' selfless today while I'm gone?"

"Like what?"

"I don't know. Walk an old lady across the street or somethin'."

Elisha followed Aaron to the front door, and Aaron stopped short and smiled.

"You know, you could have packed me a lunch. That would have been a nice selfless thing to do."

Elisha shut the door. It was kind of dangerous having someone else know that you had to work on your selflessness.

Jonathan tried his best to avoid the strange looks he was getting on all sides. His supermarket cart was piled high with ten 16-pound bags of cat food, and this was his *second* trip since yesterday. The other shoppers probably thought he ran an animal shelter. As long as none of his nosey neighbors were around he'd be fine. He got to the checkout and paid with his credit card but also couldn't help wincing at the bill again. Journalism paid well, but not *that* well. Jonathan stuffed all the bags of cat food into the black garbage bags he had bought. He really had been *so* incredibly stupid. You never transformed something outside of the Foundation Vault that couldn't be 'validated' by an outsider. He hadn't answered his door in 24 hours even when it had been the plumber that he'd been desperately waiting for every single day for over a week. One look at Stripes' size and anyone would either pass out or call in the National Enquirer. Jonathan exhaled. As bad as the situation was, he was still desperately hoping that 'Godzilla' Stripes was for real and not just in his imagination. She couldn't possibly be eating so much if she wasn't!

Devorah better get here soon. He almost wanted to text her his address, but he was afraid she'd be insulted. She knew how to find him. He lugged the black garbage bags into the elevator in two trips and then rested for a second on a kitchen chair. His entire living room was just full of cat. He tore open three bags of food and dumped them on the floor. Stripes polished them off in two minutes.

Devorah better get here today!

Elisha went back into his room and stared at his reflection in the Ispaklaria. Even though most of what the King had told him seemed fuzzy around the edges, Elisha hadn't forgotten a *word* about the reflections part. He hadn't mentioned it to Aaron because they bordered on that forbidden zone of his solemn oath to Rav Kadosh, *and* because he definitely had a very bad taste in his own mouth. And he had thought *Josh* was full of himself!? And he couldn't even bear to remember how he had shouted at Gila. He cringed. And now *what*? If he would be nice to her at this point she'd think he was crazy, and how could he ever help someone like that?

He went out to the courtyard where Gila was playing with Shira and started studying Gila quietly. He tried making a mental inventory of the damage: her face was covered with the worse acne he had seen, she was probably twice the size she should have been, her teeth were grey or something weird was wrong with them, her hair was always wet looking or maybe it was just greasy and her clothes kinda looked like . . . garbage bags. He didn't have anyone he could compare notes with, but he still got that the whole effect was *not good*. Come to think of it, he'd never even once seen her with a friend. And there was nothing on that list that he could change.

The funny thing was that Shira didn't seem to notice any of that. Shira was always *so* happy whenever Gila was around. What *was* he missing? It didn't really matter. The selfish part of him understood that Gila was an obstacle course in selflessness training. But when he thought over what he could do, he realized there wasn't a *thing*. He'd have to leave her case for advanced training some other time.

"Say bye-bye to Elisha," Gila called out and waved Shira's little hand.

Elisha was surprised that she was even speaking to him through Shira.

"Where are you going?" he asked, non-interested.

"Your mother called and asked me to get a few things from the grocery store."

That was annoying, since that was his job, but it was also opportunity number one. Elisha offered, "I can do that for you."

Gila eyed him suspiciously and said, "No. I want to buy Shira something special, but I won't know what it is until she sees it." She turned to Shira and said, "Right, cutie? So we have to go together." She gave him a condescending look. "But you can come and carry the bags *after* you apologize to me."

That wasn't what he was offering, because Elisha honestly didn't want to be seen in the same space with her. "Forget it," he said. But her next words hit him head on.

"Suit your selfish self."

And he muttered "Sorry" and set off a few paces behind them, thinking this selflessness business was seriously tough stuff.

CHAPTER SIX

Gifts of Wisdom

A TIME TO BE SILENT AND A TIME TO SPEAK

Rebecca was doing her absolute best *not* to run out of the hospital room. If she heard *that* name one more time, she was sure she would. Daniel said it again—"Paul Montgomery the third!"— and this time he said it as if he was announcing his own entry into a royal ballroom.

She started to stand up, but Daniel was so excited that he grabbed at her arm and stopped her planned escape.

"I am amazed! What do you think? I think it *was* seeing those boys. I think somehow their childhood innocence caused a latent trigger to my own childhood subconscious." He looked at her suspiciously. "Why aren't *you* excited about my breakthrough?"

"I, I am. It's just that you're not, you're Daniel *not* Paul."

Daniel immediately let go of her.

"I would appreciate if you would stop calling me that absurd name. I know my own name now! I *remembered my own name*!"

115

Rebecca looked at him with concern. On the one hand, he seemed to be having a surge of energy. But he was acting so different! *Was* this a breakthrough? He seemed like a total stranger and his eyes were so distant when he started to describe his first real memory.

"I have this image of . . . of my childhood . . . in England. I can see my house. Brick! Yes, it is made from red bricks. And everything is plush green and there are colorful flowers and I'm walking to church with my father. I'm holding his hand . . . it's a grand old church and there are beautiful stained glass windows . . . the sun is reflecting through them like a prism and I can see . . ." Daniel stopped with a face full of disappointment. "You see, that's where it ends. I woke up with this one idyllic postcard picture and that's it. Nothing more. That's it!!"

He threw his hands up in frustration and glared at Rebecca. There was an edge to his voice that Rebecca had never heard in all their years of marriage.

"*How* did I get *here?* What on earth am I doing in the Holy Land of all places? *TELL ME!*"

Rebecca said, "I'll be right back," and then ran out to the hallway and called Ezra on her cellphone.

"*Help!*"

"What happened?" he asked in alarm.

"He's telling me that he's *Paul!* He's talking about his childhood and walking to church with his father!"

There was no sound on the other end.

"*Ezra!*"

Ezra didn't understand what she was even saying, until it hit him all at once. And then he answered her excitedly. "*Rebecca, his name was Paul!* He was Paul *before* he converted."

"I know that!" she snapped.

GIFTS OF WISDOM 117

"Well then what's the matter? This is *fantastic news*! He's *finally* getting his memory back—*amazing,* and—"

"No. He's acting bizarre. It's not him. I *know* him, and it's not him."

"*Stop!* He's probably just got to work up to the part where he grows up and turns into Daniel." Ezra felt his heart beating rapidly. He *was* finally coming back. "I'll be over right away . . ."

"But what am I supposed to *say* to him in the meantime?"

"*Really,* Rebecca! Just be supportive! Call him Paul or whatever he likes. Just help him along. He must be coming back! Don't ruin it, *deal* with it!" He looked at his watch in frustration. *With traffic and parking it might take half an hour. "PLEASE just* humor him, coach him, remind him, *whatever,* and just *don't* mess this up!"

Rebecca took a deep breath and walked back into the room. Really, she wasn't handling this well at all, she chided herself. This was a breakthrough, right? His memory was coming back. She'd work alongside him tirelessly until all of him came back to her. Of course she would. Patience was a virtue. She went over to the bedside and lovingly took hold of his hand. Daniel returned it to her and said,

"Well, you don't know me as Paul. And I don't know you as Rebecca. So that should tell us both something."

Rebecca nodded her head and smiled. *Was that being supportive enough?* She didn't like the expression on his face. It was one she had never seen, and it almost made him look like a different man.

"You are undoubtedly a lovely looking woman, but you also must be a very troubled one to try and pretend that I'm your husband, when in fact you never even saw me before in your life." He clenched his jaw and looked at her with obvious disgust. "What kind of person would abduct a man and steal his identity?"

Rebecca was left with her mouth agape.

He stared at her with a foreboding look and said, "You might be many things, but you are certainly *not* a good Christian."

Rebecca's eyes widened. *What did Ezra say? I need to call him Paul! And I need to humor him.*

"Well, umm, *Paul.* You . . . are *right* and you know how . . . sometimes things aren't, they aren't sometimes *really,* not at all the way they seem?"

"I'm calling in the authorities."

Rebecca couldn't hide her shaking shoulders. She was forcing herself not to cry when Daniel let out an agonizing scream. His face seemed momentarily frozen. *Was he having a stroke?* She blamed herself—she had done a horrible job at humoring him! She was about to call for a nurse when his face relaxed and he mumbled:

"Alicia is the foundation; Alicia will bring shom-air."

Rebecca let out a long sigh of relief and took hold of his hand as he drifted off to sleep. *Those* words were at least vital life blood to her tormented heart. She immediately berated herself. She had worked herself up for nothing, because here he was talking about their beautiful new baby daughter, Alicia. He had even called her the *Yessod,* foundation, as if he meant to say that she was the foundation of their lives. How sweet, she thought to herself, that Alicia will bring 'some air'—was that what he meant? Or did he mean to say that she brings sunshine and air? That was probably it, because otherwise it sounded like '*shamir,*' which made no sense at all.

Going selflessness shopping with Gila turned out to be the biggest mistake of Elisha's summer. He was in the dairy section reaching for the 1% milk and checking his mother's list when he heard a loud barrage of horrible snorting noises. But when he turned into the next aisle, he didn't know what to do with himself. They were for *her*.

Gila was holding Shira and valiantly trying to ignore the group of teenage boys who were now oinking loudly. She was trying to stay focused on Shira, picking out a Hello Kitty lollipop from the shelf and saying, "Isn't this one pretty?" but she was wiping her eyes and then her nose with the same hand that held the lollipop.

Now the teenage boys were inter-mingling their snorts, oinks and grunts with roaring laughter. Elisha couldn't believe it. He wanted to disappear. Actually, he wanted to disappear for Gila. He looked at the floor. All she was doing in here was trying to do something nice for his own sister. He felt a rising anger, and without even thinking he rushed over to Gila and grabbed her hand. He couldn't believe he was actually touching her, or the hand that she had just used to wipe her nose, and he said loudly, "You don't belong with these *pigs,* let's go!"

The teenage boys cracked up laughing and left. Gila was still wiping her nose. In a voice that tried to mask her pain while regaining some dignity she said to Elisha, "Thanks, but you didn't have to, I'm used to it," and with that she went straight to the cashier.

How could anyone get used to *that?* Elisha wondered. He was even contemplating committing suicide *for* her.

Gila left the bags on the floor and then pointed to

them. They were heavy. Elisha took them but then also took his time to let Gila and Shira get a good block ahead of him. He couldn't help thinking in the back of his mind that thankfully he had no idea what it was like to be Gila. And then he inwardly smiled, because if this wasn't being a selfless hero then what was?

That's when a foot came out of nowhere and tripped him. The grocery bags unbalanced him, and he fell awkwardly onto the stone pathway. He didn't even have to hear the boys laughing to know how stupid he looked. His face had hit the ground with a loud smack, and he thought his cheekbone was broken. He painfully picked himself up and could see a sort of familiar face. He hadn't really looked at the boys in the store, but now there was no doubt about it. He was looking at an older version of Avshalom from his own class, who was their elementary school Mafioso. He didn't know which of Avshalom's brothers it was, but he knew there were six. Every one of them was a factory reproduction of the same bad model, just in different sizes. Apparently the family could only manufacture the same personalities too, because Avshalom model X was now grabbing his whole body and picking him up.

Elisha heard one of the boys to the side saying, "Come on Yoav, leave him alone. He's just a kid." But the Avshalom-look-alike Yoav wasn't satisfied.

"Hey look at this, he's so lightweight, he's like air." And to prove it, Yoav swung Elisha a full 360 degrees and then said in a mocking dorky voice, "Isn't your girlfriend a little BIG for you."

That elicited snickering all around.

Elisha felt seasick. He could have cried from the pain on his cheek, and now his T-shirt was cutting into

GIFTS OF WISDOM 121

his neck and choking him, but he didn't dare cry. The square thick face now held him up so their faces were on the same level.

"You know, you're a lot prettier than she is, so you know what? I might even let you go after you say you're sorry. But you gotta say it like you *mean* it."

Elisha was thinking the ugly big *pig* could knock him senseless and he wouldn't give him the satisfaction of hearing those two words. But why couldn't he think of even *one* smart thing to do to get out of it? Couldn't just a speck of King Solomon's wisdom have rubbed off on him? And it occurred to him that selflessness was not only really dangerous, it could even be fatal.

The older version of Avshalom grabbed Elisha by the throat and said, "Hey, I'm waiting. And look at me when I'm talking to you."

Fear gripped Elisha. He felt he could barely breathe as he looked straight into Avshalom X's beady eyes. Black eyes with a red reflection. Black eyes that were turning red. Elisha didn't mistake the red reflection this time. *Avshalom-X was also one of those red-shadowed, broken, non-deserving people.* He was Gila all over again! Elisha *saw* it! But could he really even try to help this red-shadowed person who was about to pulverize him? And maybe it *would* be better if Avshalom-X *did* commit suicide, and right about now, because it was definitely a *good* time for him to go. A sharp pain seared through Elisha's head. And then a worse nausea took a hold of his body. It was *knowing*. It was not wanting to know, but somehow knowing what it felt like to be Yoav. Elisha nearly choked. And then, without thinking, he even said them—the two words "I'm sorry"—because he did feel sorry. He suddenly felt really sorry for him. At this rate, Avshalom X would probably live most of his life behind bars. Elisha didn't break his stare, and when he said it again, he really meant it, and the words came out *in stereo*.

"I'm sorry," said Avshalom's brother, and he set Elisha back on the ground.

Elisha blinked his eyes, maybe he hadn't heard *right?* But now his bags were being picked up for him and Avshalom's brother was scuffing up his hair.

Yoav couldn't quite understand it, but when he looked into the scrawny kid's big blue eyes something made him feel connected to the little wimp. The kid understood him. And hey, he had learned his lesson, and that was the point. He looked down at the cut on Elisha's face and asked, "Are you OK?"

Elisha thought that his face was probably broken in half, but he still waved his hand dismissively and said, "Yeah, I'm OK."

Yoav sneered to himself. The kid was so girly looking, he'd never last a day on the street. He squinted his eyes at Elisha. "Do you have a big brother?"

Elisha shook his head no.

Yoav's black eyes opened wide. Looking straight at him, he said, "Now you do."

Great, Elisha thought as he headed home quickly trying to figure out *what in the world* had happened. All he knew was that seeing inside Yoav's head made him feel sick to his stomach. It was like contracting a disease of painful memories. If *that* was a gift of wisdom, Elisha preferred amnesia.

"What took you so *long?*" Gila complained. Then she saw Elisha's face and immediately turned angry and worried at the same time. "Great! Look what you did to yourself. You shouldn't have started up with *them!*"

Elisha rushed over to inspect his face in the mirror near the front door. His cheek had a big cut and was red and swollen all around. It really did look like he had just been in a bad fight. He said defensively, "I just fell."

Gila didn't buy it for a second. "Yeah, right," she scoffed as she rushed to the bathroom and quickly brought back a soapy warm washcloth. "I can't believe you started up with kids twice your age!"

Elisha was offended. "They're not *twice* my age."

Gila snorted, "They're 15, OK, I know. They're my age."

Elisha winced as she tried to gently clean the cut. "I'm almost 11, so they're not!"

Gila was talking out loud, "Your parents are going to *kill* me."

He shoved her hand off his face with an, "Ouch. You're killing me with this."

Gila seemed frantic and fretted, "They're going to *kill* me for not taking better care of you!"

Elisha grabbed the washcloth out of her hand, and said, "*Stop!* Okay, you're not *my* babysitter."

"Oh yes, I am."

After losing his way five times in a maze of tiny alleyways in Jerusalem's Old City, Dr. Brody found himself in the waiting room of Rabbi Isaac Abrahamson. He had come highly recommended by his secretary Keren, who had personally read all of his Kabbalah books and couldn't stop going *on and on* about him. Dr. Brody had barely patted the sweat off his forehead with a disposable anti-bacterial wipe when the rabbi personally came out of his study to invite him in. He was surprised to see that the rabbi was a clean-shaven redhead, wearing regular clothes and in his mid-forties—not that age was a requirement for knowledge, but Dr. Brody had inwardly been hoping to see some aged white-bearded personage who might possess that mysterious Dalai Lama insight into Jonathan's bizarre visions.

"Thank you for agreeing to see me on such short notice, Rabbi Abrahamson."

The friendly face shook his hand, offered him a seat and a cold glass of water, and asked, "So, how can I help?"

Dr. Brody really doubted he'd be able to and was thinking that for starters an air-conditioned underground parking lot with an elevator would be good; but having come as far as Jerusalem, he certainly had to give him a try. "Well, I'll get right to the point. I'm treating a patient who has . . . out-of-the ordinary visions. He sees images of multi-dimensional animal heads with thousands of wings that he calls a *Merkavah*. He's always talking about Sephirot, which he describes as nothing. He sees hundreds of gates and marble hallways with waves. He mentions names like Enoch and Metatron, and even once chanted *abracadabra*."

Having never discussed the case with anyone before, Dr. Brody suddenly realized how absurd he sounded. But the rabbi seemed unfazed, and so Dr. Brody pursued the subject. "So, Rabbi Abrahamson, what in your opinion would be the basis for those kinds of bizarre hallucinations?"

Rabbi Abrahamson did raise an eyebrow, even

GIFTS OF WISDOM   125

though it was ever so slight, and then answered, "Those images are all from the realm of Kabbalah, Jewish mysticism, although some of them are in the Bible in the first chapter of the Book of Ezekiel."

Dr. Brody was surprised that the young rabbi hadn't hesitated a second in identifying the outrageous references. It made him feel like he wasn't well read, and in point of fact, in Jewish areas, he wasn't. But had he really missed something that was in the Bible? That was embarrassing; after all it was still an all-time bestseller.

Rabbi Abrahamson continued, "Although some of the items you mentioned would be attributed to the period of the Talmud, and particularly Rabbi Akiva's time, right after the destruction of the Second Temple around 2000 years ago."

Dr. Brody was nodding, but, honestly, he didn't know much about Rabbi Akiva besides the name. "And how does any of *this* relate to the *Talmud?*"

Rabbi Abrahamson's face brightened. "Ah! Well! Just about *anything* and *everything* that has to do with Kabbalah will lead you back to the Talmud." He looked straight into Dr. Brody's eyes, hesitated slightly and then continued with a lowered voice. "You see, there's a strange passage in 'Chagigah, tractate 14b' known as *Arba Nichnasu LaPardes*, that tells a very important story about 'four people who entered a *pardes* or orchard."

Dr. Brody almost rolled his eyes—what was this man going on about orchards for? He tried not to show his annoyance while the rabbi continued.

"But the 'orchard' wasn't *really* an orchard. Let's just say it was a cryptic name for an other-worldly dimension—or in your profession, a different state of consciousness."

At that, Dr. Brody immediately became intrigued. He was also surprised that the Talmud would have anything so esoteric; he had always thought it was just a monstrous tome of laws. "Would you mind giving me more details on this particular passage?" Dr. Brody asked.

"Well the four that entered the '*pardes*' were actually four giants, or I should say gifted geniuses, of the Talmudic period. They were the greatest minds of their time, if not of *all* time. In a sense, they were among the first Kabbalah masters, and their names were Rabbi Akiva, Simeon Ben Azai, Simeon Ben Zoma and Elisha ben Abuyah."

Dr. Brody couldn't have cared less about their names, and immediately moved the conversation back on track. "And what did they do in this . . . this orange grove?"

Rabbi Abrahamson repeated, "*Pardes*—orchard. It could even be a cryptic name for the Garden of Eden, but definitely not an orange grove."

All Dr. Brody could think was, *here's another nitpicker.* But he remained attentive while Rabbi Abrahamson breathed in deeply.

"Well . . . the story goes that they used some kind of mystical technique that enabled them to gain access to divine chambers—basically, an entirely separate reality from our own."

There was that 'chambers' trigger word. Dr. Brody became excitedly impatient. "Yes, yes, and so what happened?"

Rabbi Abrahamson was hesitant. "Well, it's not a happily-ever-after story. After visiting the highest chamber, Simeon Ben Azai died, Simeon ben Zoma lost his mind and Elisha ben Abuyah became a heretic. In fact, his name was deleted from the entire Talmud afterward and

GIFTS OF WISDOM

replaced with the name *Acher* or 'The Other."

Again, Dr. Brody couldn't have cared less about these name factoids, but he was curious about the one name he recognized. "And Rabbi Akiva?"

"Oh, sorry, he's the hero of the story. He entered in peace and left in peace."

At that, Dr. Brody could tell that Rabbi Abrahamson had finished, but he was still hungry for more. "And that's it?? What about all the wings, marble and waves?"

That question seemed to fluster Rabbi Abrahamson, and he answered, "Well, quite honestly, it's not even the tip of the iceberg. You're inquiring about a subject that has an enormous amount of writing, and much of it is so highly esoteric that even the best of scholars are clueless."

Dr. Brody sighed to himself. *A disappointing dead end.* Still he tried: "Well, isn't there some kind of definitive summary that one can read up on?"

"Believe me, Dr. Brody, even if you dedicated the rest of your life to researching it, you wouldn't get very far."

"But doesn't that same Talmudic passage tell you at least what actually transpired in this *'pardes'?* " he asked using the right word carefully.

"*Hardly.* The fact that it's even recorded in the Talmud at all is essentially a warning *never* to even try it!" Rabbi Abrahamson turned very serious. "You're not supposed to mess around with altered consciousness or to try to—I don't know—beam yourself into some different dimension. If three out of the four of these great men didn't make it, then it's a lesson to us mere mortals to stay clear of the whole practice. However, if you're so very curious to find out where your patient is getting his source material from, you might want to get hold of the *Heichalot* or 'Chambers' literature—"

"Chambers Literature??"

Rabbi Abrahamson was already writing down reference for him and saying, "Yes, it will give you a full account of the mystical journeys of the Talmudic sages during their seven-stage ascent into the higher realms. It's replete with the images you mentioned, and it will give you lots of 'scenic' details of what went on in the *pardes*. You'll find all your marble, wings and waves in there . . ." he smiled, "and a lot more."

Dr. Brody leaned back in his chair. This information was key. It meant that Jonathan's visions were not original. He could have easily accessed all of this strange imagery from the same source that Rabbi Abrahamson had just mentioned. He focused back on the question that was foremost in his mind.

"Rabbi Abrahamson, would it all be possible for groups of people to be studying these subjects?"

"Sure, millions, as well as myself."

Shocked, Dr. Brody exclaimed, "You mean to tell me you have these visions as well?"

At that Rabbi Abrahamson quickly said, "*Absolutely not!*" and explained: "Kabbalah is divided into three separate areas—theory, meditation and practice. We study the *theory—only!* Which is basically a religious philosophy."

Dr. Brody relaxed a little and said, "I see . . . so, for heaven's sake, what *is* this *practical* Kabbalah then?"

Rabbi Abrahamson leaned back in his chair and said, "Well, I guess you could think of it as a kind of white magic. It's sort of an ancient wisdom that uses a variety of techniques that supposedly enable an individual to have supernatural powers."

Dr. Brody was almost on the edge of his own seat when he asked, "Supernatural powers?? What kind of

GIFTS OF WISDOM 129

techniques??"

Rabbi Abrahamson rattled off, "Historically, lots—use of Divine names, incantations, amulets, talismans, and you'd also find chiromancy, physiognomy and astrology."

Dr. Brody couldn't help jumping at the word incantations. He quickly remarked, "Yes, my patient is continuously mumbling all sorts of idiotic and incoherent syllables in insufferably long chants. It's quite comical, believe me."

"I can understand how it must *sound* ridiculous, but then you're missing a vital point. You see, in practical Kabbalah the letters of the Hebrew alphabet are really the foundation for *everything*, or at least for the 'magic' part."

"How did they get to *that?*"

"Well, it's based on the Bible. At each stage in the creation of the universe, the Bible introduces the account by stating, 'And God said' . . ."

Dr. Brody was delighted to have the opportunity to show that he wasn't a total ignoramus and he quickly recited one of the only sections of the Bible that he was familiar with. "Yes, of course, and God said let there be light, land, animals, etcetera . . . *So?*"

"So, creation took place through *words*. And words of course consist of letters, and that's why the letters of the Hebrew alphabet are the most basic building blocks of creation. You said your patient chanted *Abracadabra*. Well, that simply means 'I will create as I speak.'"

Dr. Brody had gotten the 'abracadabra' lesson from Jonathan already, but still asked if Rabbi Abrahamson could elaborate.

"I know it's difficult to comprehend, but you need to understand that Hebrew isn't considered a conventional language. In other languages, if everyone decides that a cat is called a cat, then that's what it is. But according to our tradition, each Hebrew word is a unique combination of sound vibrations that actually communicates the essence, or let's even say the molecular structure, of the object that it represents." Rabbi Abrahamson got up from his desk. "Actually, to understand practical Kabbalah you're better off being a math, chemist or physics genius."

Dr. Brody didn't like the 'Professor Bezalel' ring to that one, and asked, "Why in the world would I need to be a physics genius to understand something 2000 years old?"

"Good question, and one that I honestly don't have the answer to, but that's how it is."

Dr. Brody sighed, "Could you just give me the laymen's version?"

"Well, I once taught a brilliant scientist and he offered me the following explanation: Think of the letters as symbols in advanced scientific formulas, and then you can partly understand it. You see, the easiest way is to think of it all as chemistry," Rabbi Abrahamson said as he waved his hands animatedly. "You know how a chemist puts the right substances or elements into a solution in order to create a new formula? Okay, so if you can stretch your imagination, think of the letters as different chemical ingredients, or even elements in the periodic table, and when each one is carefully measured out and combined the right way with others then you've created a new formula, right? Even Coca-Cola gets created that way. So you see the letter chants are doing the same thing, they're manipulating the letters which are the chemicals or the basic elements of creation. And there you have it—magic."

Dr. Brody laughed. It was the most preposterous

GIFTS OF WISDOM

thing he had ever heard. He couldn't believe that the intelligent-looking man sitting across from him had even repeated it. "And do you actually believe this nonsensical tripe—sorry, I mean these myths?"

Rabbi Abrahamson didn't respond, and Dr. Brody rephrased himself. He really needed to get to his *real* question. "Sorry, but would it at all be possible for, I mean *are* there people out there who actually think they're doing it?"

Now it was Rabbi Abrahamson's turn to laugh. "I'm sorry," he said and laughed some more. "I'm sorry I didn't make myself clearer from the start. Practical Kabbalah doesn't exist."

"What?" Dr. Brody looked at him utterly confused.

"The practical side or magical side of Kabbalah is *lost*. It's an ancient, incomprehensible wisdom, and no one can say for sure if it *ever* really worked to begin with. It's more the stuff of legends and storytelling. And you should also know that from a rabbinical point of view, it was always considered such a highly dangerous discipline that the rabbis banned it altogether, *ages* ago. Even just studying *theoretical* Kabbalah before the age of 40 was prohibited. So as you can imagine, the practical side or the 'white magic' part always had to be hidden away in secret societies, and that meant that the only way it could be passed down through the generations was by individuals—very cryptically, you know by a master or teacher to his student or disciple, that sort of thing. And because of that, you won't find any instruction manuals. Most of the practical Kabbalah manuscripts that did survive through time are so abstruse and obscure that they're entirely undecipherable."

Dr. Brody made a mental note of the 'master-disciple'

method, and then asked, "Are you absolutely *sure?*"

Rabbi Abrahamson said, "Look, I'm sure you could find some kind of crackpot," he corrected himself, "sorry, a highly unstable individual who might think he can try, like your patient, I guess. But then as a psychiatrist, I'm sure you're in your own element as to what to call it. Psychotic? Delusional? Or is it Jerusalem Syndrome?"

Rav Kadosh was deep in thought. Why hadn't the boy received the *Shamir* YET? Nothing would ever amount to anything if they didn't have the *Shamir*. He carefully turned the parchment page of the ancient starscript manuscript he was reading and then stared at his desk. Even after decades of dedicating his life to the study of Torah and Kabbalah, he honestly didn't even have the slightest notion of what the *Shamir* was or even what it looked like. Although he certainly understood its significance! Rav Kadosh pushed aside the morning newspaper that someone had left on his desk. Why did all the headlines always seem more or less the same? One way or another, they always seemed to suggest that the world was getting one step closer to World War III. Rav Kadosh sighed. 'Kabbalah' simply meant 'receiving', but the only message he was receiving was that the boy was somehow going to be instrumental in *receiving* the *Shamir*. So *where* was it? It was already painfully obvious that the *Yessod* was simply a selfish child who thought everything was one big game. Rav Kadosh dropped his head into his hands. He wasn't sure if he'd be able to survive more than two to three meetings with the boy. He shook his head sorrowfully and thought of Daniel Bezalel. The man was a raging radical in his opinion, one who threw all caution to the winds. Point of fact—he hadn't even survived his first encounter with the *Yessod*. *One who plays with fire will eventually be burned by it.* They probably all would. Certainly counting on a pampered and spoiled child to achieve even the lowest level of selflessness in order to merit receiving the *Shamir,* was completely unrealistic. In any case, what could a child of that age and social standing even *do* that would ever count, when he probably thought folding his own clothes made him a superhero. He hoped the *Yessod* was enjoying his summer vacation while the Eighth Kingdom continued to totter precariously.

"He started up with a *group* of boys *twice* his age!"

That was the whole conversation around supper. Gila managed to get it in four times, Elisha had counted, and each time she said it with increased exasperation. His parents thought they were keeping their grave looks to themselves. But Elisha felt their disappointment hanging so thick over the dinner table that he could barely take his eyes off the inedible food on his plate. The first time Gila had said it, Aaron had laughed and said with gusto, "Good for you! How bad do the other kids look?" But the disapproval in the air was so tangible that Aaron immediately filled his mouth with double portions of food to shut himself up.

After a while, all Elisha could hear around the table was chewing. Gila was a traitor, a non-deserving, red-shadowed traitor, and she chewed the loudest. But he didn't say anything. And much as he would have loved to tell the *whole* story, he wasn't going to . . . not even Gila deserved that, and definitely not for the sake of what, making him*self* look good? Elisha stole a glance at Shira in her high chair. What was left of the Hello Kitty lollipop was now glued to her bib. And since her vocabulary consisted of about three words, he was sure that the whole thing would go down to the grave.

"They're the roughest kids in the neighborhood too," Gila thoughtfully added to the silence.

Now was definitely one of the moments when Elisha wished he could disappear like this morning. Maybe he could just stare at them all and they'd suddenly say they were sorry. But that would mean making eye contact, and he definitely didn't want to give anyone an unobstructed frontal view of his swollen red, black and blue face.

Aaron knew that it would be best to avoid Elisha. He was 'dead kid walkin' until his parents got through with him. He went straight into the kitchen and rolled up his sleeves to be the first one to wash up the dishes. When Elisha cleared off the table and set a pile of plates by the sink, Aaron quickly whispered, "What happened?"

Elisha, scraped the food into the garbage and said, "It's okay. It's a selflessness injury."

Aaron smiled and whispered, "Thatta boy!"

But his time was up. An ominous voice drifted in from the kitchen doorway and said with too much calm restraint, "Elisha, I want to speak with you in your room please."

The first thing that came out of his father's mouth was a long exhale and then, "I want you to be a person of substance. Do you understand the meaning of substance, Elisha? It means that I want you to be a person that uses his mind—brains, not brawn."

Elisha studied the tile on the floor that looked like a fish with a mustache while his father continued.

GIFTS OF WISDOM   135

"Can you name even *one* thing that you've done this entire summer that has had any real significance or substance?"

Well, Elisha had found an Ispaklaria, a *Choshen* stone, and a direct descendant of Aaron, and had even met *King Solomon.*

His father wasn't really waiting for an answer and said, "I thought not." He sighed heavily again. "Do you have *anything* to say for yourself about starting up with boys twice your age??"

Elisha thought silently to himself. *They weren't twice my age, and I was trying to help Gila's sorry red-shadowed suicidal self, and that's what I'm still doing now by not telling you about it.*

"I thought not." His father raised his eyes to the ceiling. "Let me ask you something else. Did you even consider the possibility of setting out one infinitesimal goal for yourself this summer?"

I'm trying to work on my selflessness. And I think I've got something important I have to do on the 9th of Av.

The absence of sound in the room was deafening.

His father stood up. "You're grounded for a week. That means you're not allowed *out* of this house for anything. No soccer, no friends, zero entertainment for you. So, don't even ask. The only time you're going out the door of this house is if your mother or I allow it. And that would *only* be for a very good reason or worthy cause." He looked directly at Elisha and said, "Needless to say, your mother and I are extremely disappointed at your behavior. "And . . ." he hesitated and then coughed, "and . . . I hope that you'll see this not so much as a punishment but as an opportunity to work on yourself." Jessie almost winced saying that last line. He had promised Tamar that he'd phrase it that way, but honestly it sounded so ridiculous.

Elisha made a quick calculation. At least he would be safely released from prison a good week before the 9th of Av. The punishment could have been worse. In any case, he had everything he needed to 'work on himself' right here at home. Maybe it was even a 'good opportunity.'

CHAPTER SEVEN

Playing with Fire

**A TIME TO PLANT
AND A TIME TO UPROOT THE PLANTED**

It was dark, but they still took the car to Tel Aviv. Akiva had insisted, and that only irked Devorah more—it was such a waste of time—until she realized he wanted to 'talk'. They were supposed to 'talk'. After they had announced their engagement, Professor Bezalel had made them both promise that they would never read each other's minds. They had agreed and understood. It was the only way they'd ever maintain any semblance of future matrimonial bliss and a peaceful marriage.

Akiva was straightforward. "I owe you two apologies . . . and you have no idea how I've been berating myself since yesterday. The way I grabbed that diary away from you was total control freak . . . and, I can't even *believe* what I said to you afterward about . . . Jonathan, and especially in front of Principal Oholiov."

He hadn't even started the car, and Devorah was ready to forgive all. But Akiva wasn't finished.

"I'm having such a hard time forgiving myself that I don't expect you to right away either. But, I wanted you to

137

know. It's not who I am or who I want to be." He shook his head. "You know, a person spends years working on himself, and just when you think you've made great headway, everything goes flying out the window . . . just hearing his name did that to me. I'm so sorry, Devorah."

The balmy breeze of the Judean Hills lulling through the windows also had a magical way of clearing the air. Before they knew it, they weren't just talking; they were laughing their heads off remembering all types of funny things that had happened in the Chambers. It also became pretty apparent that so many of their memories included Jonathan.

"We were *all* jealous of him, *I* was always jealous of him, until . . . Do you remember that time he beat me in the Chambers memory tournament?"

Devorah laughed. "Yeah, a 1,000-letter-long permutation! He probably cheated."

"No. He was better. But I'll never forget how Professor Bezalel took me to the side afterwards. He told me, 'Akiva. No one and no thing can *ever* take anything away from you if it was meant to be yours. Nothing on this earth has that much power. If you don't get something you've wanted, it means that the One never meant for you to have it. Nothing you can do will change that.'" He looked at her and added, "I accept that wholeheartedly."

Devorah felt tortured. Another mystery of the universe—she was never more certain of her choice than when he was selfless enough to let her go! She knew how Jonathan had a way of overshadowing everyone around him in the Chambers; his whole Fifth Dimensional self consisted of a self-centered perfectionism rather than truly perfecting himself. It was true that Jonathan had been the smartest, the quickest, the best looking, the most creative, the most powerful . . . but he was the absolute worst where it counted! She turned to Akiva and said, "But how could you ever be jealous of *him* when you're the *whole*hearted one and he's entirely heart*less*!"

Akiva pointed to the windshield and drew into the air the first letter in his name—an '*ayin*'—and then drew the first letter of Devorah's name—a '*daled*'. The letters reached the nighttime sky outlined in silvery twinkling stars. He waited. Devorah did the same, placing her constellation right next to his. The two Hebrew words now spelled out 'Until Eternity.'

They both smiled.

While Akiva parked the car, he also assured her, "If he's not in *tohu v'bohu*, I won't have any part of *karet* either."

Jonathan perceived Devorah's presence the minute she set foot in the apartment building. He immediately felt a deep sense of relief—until he also detected Akiva following in her footsteps, or more like bonded to her very being. He realized that he shouldn't have expected otherwise, and that he wasn't in any position to call the shots.

The minute he let them through the door, he also realized they were firewalling their minds. *Have it your way* . . .they would communicate through speech and it would take a hundred times longer. At this point, all Jonathan really cared about was whether they could 'validate' Godzilla Stripes or not.

Except that once the three were in the same enclosed space, they couldn't help but take a moment to study each other's essence. It had been a long time. Jonathan couldn't help noting that none of Devorah's online photos did even minimal justice to the real thing. But as for Akiva, he was more boring and self-righteous-looking than ever—*a sanctimonious goody-seven-shoes*. Devorah instantly gained the perspective she hadn't had as a teenager. She had always looked up to Jonathan, and now she was looking down. It was sobering, but it felt great to be set free from an old illusion. Akiva felt a sudden pang of regret. Why hadn't he ever tried to help Jonathan? It was so obvious that his destructive nature was also self-consuming. Why stand idly by? They all broke their stares at the same time.

Devorah was cool-headed and had the situation assessed in seconds. She was looking at a Chamber Five initiate who was debilitated by Chamber Five *tohu v'bohu*. And you didn't need to be a Fifth Dimensional Luminary to figure out what Jonathan wanted to 'validate' either. There were at least ten empty bags of cat food strewn across the living room and a mountain's worth of food that looked untouched.

Akiva nodded at Devorah and she returned the nod. There were no shortcuts. *Tohu v'bohu* needed to be substantiated 100%. Beyond reasonable doubt wasn't good enough. There were two ways of going about it, the hard way or easy way. Devorah tried the easy way first. She turned to Jonathan and said, "Let me in." She only needed one second in Jonathan's mind to verify his reality. Of course, in that one second she was also adept enough to glean at least a month's worth of Jonathan's most intimate thoughts. As she expected, Jonathan's response was an adamant, "Never."

Akiva knew she didn't have a chance. There were very few men willing to bare their souls, period, and baring it to an X chromosome wasn't particularly up there . . . *especially if she was the most beautiful woman*

PLAYING WITH FIRE 141

on earth. Akiva knew he would have to try. "Then let *me* in."

Jonathan laughed hysterically and stared at Stripes. His heart felt like it was being wrenched out of his body. He didn't even get the chance to ask them to 'validate' her and they were already commencing *tohu v'bohu* validation protocol. Jonathan spat out venomously, "My cat takes up the *entire* living room. Feel free to do all your dirty work from there, but just get the show on the road already."

Devorah and Akiva exchanged glances. They needed to perform an all-out assault on three of Jonathan's senses precisely from the exact area where his *tohu v'bohu* hallucinations were emanating. It was the only method to verify if an initiate was totally out of touch with reality. If Jonathan's senses didn't react to whatever spectacular 'show' they conjured, they could be 100% sure that *tohu v'bohu* had taken over his mind.

Devorah went right to work. She took two minutes to buffer Jonathan's entire apartment and seal it off from sight and sound. She then nodded to Akiva. She knew he didn't possess the most creative imagination, but she was sure that whatever he chose would be adequate. She also wanted to give him the honors.

Akiva was fast. He instantly exploded a miniature F15 fighter plane straight into the living room. The entire apartment shook violently. Every window was blown out. The steel girding in the living room walls was dangling precariously, while the floor looked like it would collapse any second. Devorah and Akiva had been thrown against the kitchen wall from the back blast. They struggled to their feet, choking violently, while trying to protect their ears and eyes. Akiva wasted no time annihilating the fireball and restoring order from the wreckage.

Jonathan hadn't flinched, but he was watching them with apprehension. What had Akiva done? Probably something ridiculously overboard compared to his super-sized fluffy housecat. He felt his eyelids twitching. He hadn't seen a thing except for Devorah and Akiva's sensory reflexes, which were . . . undeniable. *It was over.*

A deathly silence hung in the room. Jonathan knew that they were both staring at him. Now all that was left was to try and hide the depths of his utter despair. He turned to Devorah and asked with as much dignity as he could muster, "Do you know how? Or do I need to wait for Professor Bezalel to stop being comatose?"

Despite what they knew about Jonathan, they couldn't help feeling sick to their stomachs. Once a person evolved a Fifth Dimensional self, cutting them off felt as grotesquely evil and cruel as blinding an artist or amputating every finger off a pianist.

Devorah spoke up softly. "I can . . . tomorrow in the Foundation Vault."

Jonathan let out a nasty snort. "Well, if I had access to the vault, I wouldn't be in this situation to begin with."

"Don't be so sure, brother," Akiva offered with a surge of heartfelt empathy.

Jonathan hatefully spat out, "Never call me *that!*"

Devorah quickly interceded with the number one question that was eating away at her. "How did *this* happen?"

Jonathan knew she wasn't asking about the *tohu v'bohu*. He responded vindictively, "Yours truly with a little help from hypnosis."

Akiva laughed out some air while Devorah sarcastically said, "Right."

Devorah reminded herself that she was talking to a pathological liar. Even if Jonathan had as many sessions as there were hours of Chambers training, *and if he could have afforded it,* hypnosis would never have triggered empowerment. Some*thing* or some*one* else had obviously helped him along.

Jonathan shot a nasty glare at Akiva. "Why is that so hard to believe? You're living proof that there's no exclusivity on wisdom."

Akiva quickly retorted, "Or, in your case, stupidity."

Jonathan immediately hurled a chair with enough force to throw Akiva right through the window. Akiva effortlessly dodged it. And then, without moving the slightest muscle, he pinned Jonathan to the floor so tightly that he could have been surgically attached to it.

Devorah grabbed Akiva's arm and said, "Let's go," and they walked out of the apartment.

Despite the humiliating position, Jonathan couldn't help smiling. It felt fantastic to be exposed to so much raw power. He'd return it one day too, three-fold. Except that for now, all he could see was the floor and a single clear message in his mind that Devorah had sent him. *Meet US at the Wall tomorrow morning at 6:00 a.m.* She had even shaped it into a lifesaver. Cute touch. It made him want to puke. They weren't going to steal his legacy. He'd just have to plan out everything very carefully and find a way to overpower the 'dynamic duo' in the Foundation Vault.

The room was roughly circular, the ceiling was low. The walls were dark black, but they never blocked out the light of the Fifth Dimensional Luminaries. This was the first time that there were three of them in one place since last summer. They weren't in the place they were supposed to be. They weren't in the Foundation Vault. She wanted to join them, but they were already gone. The only one she found was *The Other* and he was crying. He wasn't crying on the outside, but he was crying on the inside and she suddenly felt like crying too when she knew what they wanted to do. *Karet* could only come from the Supernal Universe. They weren't allowed to do it. Not to a Seven. He was once a Seven. He would be a Seven again. That made him a Seven. She saw that he was still in *tohu v'bohu*. She wondered if she could help him. She wondered if she should help him. The *Yessod* had helped him.

She laid out the chaos and void in his mind and studied it carefully. She saw exactly what he was missing. It was a very bad thing to be missing and she wondered how to fix his *tohu v'bohu* without doing something that would be very very bad. She decided she would have to make sure to set before his eyes what he should have been seeing at all times, *always*. If he didn't see it, if he still blocked it out, if he still kept it missing, then he would be forced to face his own dark shadows instead. She watched inside *The Other*'s mind as she healed all of his *tohu v'bohu*. It was gone now—every last bit. She only hoped that he wouldn't ignore the shadows that she left him. After all, they were a gift.

Jonathan stayed stuck to the floor until Devorah and Akiva had left the city limits of Tel Aviv. As he peeled himself off, he had the strange sensation that someone had intruded on him. He searched the apartment. The living room was empty. What had happened to Stripes? Jonathan didn't dwell on her disappearance; he was just elated

PLAYING WITH FIRE

to get his space back. He looked at his watch. If things didn't go well tomorrow, he only had nine hours left to live it up, and Jonathan had no intention of squandering even a minute of that time. But he did need to choose wisely. There were a million places he would have loved to transport himself in his *tohu v'bohu* state and hundreds of great fantasy books he could have dropped himself into. But he also knew that it was extremely dangerous to get carried away. He might miss his appointment in the Foundation Vault.

He'd have to limit his transformations to the confines of his own familiar apartment. Nothing extravagant and nothing out of the norm . . . Something that wouldn't make him lose track of too much time. He breathed in deeply and let his mind relax and then just went with the flow . . . .

A ten course candle-lit dinner for two appeared on his table with gold cloches doming each plate. Silver ice buckets appeared, holding bottles of expensive champagne. He turned one of his walls into a trellis and covered it with hundreds of fresh snow-white roses. The adjoining wall became a floor-to-ceiling aquarium that he filled with white sea horses and angelfish. The music he conjured was soft, yet so flawless that it could have been a live performance. His finishing touch was a graceful floor-to-ceiling gazebo that he filled with a dozen pure-white doves. After dusting himself off, he dressed in a tuxedo and studied his reflection. Perfect. Then he tried to imagine the most beautiful white dress on earth for his soon-to-be company. He was surprised to see that his shimmering, intricate pearl-and-lace creation resembled a wedding dress. He was about to search online for her photo when his doorbell buzzed. Jonathan wasn't fazed.

He had no problem opening the door now, since it was all in his mind and there was absolutely nothing to hide. The minute he saw who was buzzing, he unlocked the door as quickly as possible. The plumber had thankfully come back!

The large, overweight middle-aged man stepped into the apartment wearing the dirtiest overalls Jonathan had ever seen and then let out an ear-piercing whistle.

"Oooh la la . . . what's the BIG occasion, buddy?"

Jonathan cocked his head to the side ever so carefully and stared hard at the man's expression.

"Who's the lucky gal? Huh?" he asked as his eyes focused on the table and then he sniffed the air coarsely. Jonathan followed the plumber's eyes and watched them stop at the dress. He suddenly slapped Jonathan gruffly on the back and said, "I guess there's about to be a *Mrs.* Marks in 6A? Ha, ha, ha."

Jonathan started laughing uncontrollably along with him. But, once the plumber found his way into the bathroom, Jonathan's validation ecstasy started to plummet. *They lied. They actually lied!* The whole thing was a staged setup. They didn't validate Stripes so they could entrap him in the Foundation Vault and do what? A dangerous unbridled fury arose in Jonathan's mind. Once the plumber and his dirty overalls were safely out the door, Jonathan unleashed a Carrie-style inferno in his apartment. His eyes lit up as he watched the conflagration. The white dress incinerated the fastest. The white roses smoldered ever so slowly. The aquarium was left untouched, but as the water heated up, every living thing in it went belly-up. And the white doves—well, they gave off the pungent aroma of a mouth-watering barbecue.

After the night's entertainment was over, Jonathan went right to work on his new fantasy—devising schemes that could give him, a single Five, the upper hand against *two* Sevens in the Foundation Vault. He settled on one plan in particular and called upon his photographic memory to search through *Shoshan Yessod Olam*, 'The Rose, Foundation of the Universe,' an old manuscript he had found at the Hebrew Literature Archives Institute. It contained over two thousand mystical formulas, but not a *single one* on how to drastically change your appearance. He mentally flipped through another one of his finds, *Toledot Adam*, 'Generations of Adam.' It had seven mystical seals that could strengthen empowerment, but nothing specific on how to unite yourself with another individual to take on their appearance. He was still only allowed into the lower halls, and even with the angelic seals he couldn't gain the required wisdom. He ended his session disgusted and frustrated. Only Professor Bezalel had seemed to know how to take all the ancient formulas to their next level—his breakthroughs made those powerful manuscripts seem primitive.

Jonathan knew that his Foundation Vault appointment was getting critically closer. But he had absolutely no intention of facing them without an advantage. He was fairly sure that his main problem in making the transformation was simply because he was incapable of unifying himself with that . . . Dudley-Do-Right-Buzzy-Light-Year pilot. He tried again. He attached his entire thought and innermost being to Akiva's essence and became deeply engulfed in finding the proper unifications. He grinned to himself before carefully positioning himself and thought, *to infinity and beyond.*

It was a long, laborious process; and after it was over, he was still 100% Jonathan Marks. As he double-checked the mirror at his side, he couldn't help loving what he saw. It was certainly better than looking at Akiva Ra'am's face. What he didn't like, was seeing that black shadow *again*. He'd first noticed it last night, after the fire was extinguished. It seemed that every time he got close to anything that was slightly reflective, there was a shadowy presence that he could see out of the corner of his eye. At first he'd thought it was his eyes playing tricks on him from exhaustion, but apparently it was constant. He'd have to do his best to ignore it.

Jonathan showered and drank three cups of coffee in a row and then topped it off with two energy drinks. He checked his watch. 6:00 a.m. had come and was long gone. He was glad that he had the foresight not to cancel his weekly appointment with Dr. Brody this morning. It was still his best chance to regain his Chamber Seven memories and access the vault by *himself*. As he rode down the elevator, wearing the darkest sunglasses he owned, he could still see the shadow covering part of his face in the elevator's mirror. It was definitely getting darker.

Akiva was disgusted when he entered Ezra's office. "We waited two whole hours, and he didn't even bother to show up."

Ezra made a steeple with his fingers and then leaned back in his chair. "Well, forgive me if I don't grieve, especially when they come and take him away . . ."

"Don't be so sure," Devorah warned.

PLAYING WITH FIRE   149

"With *tohu v'bohu*? Don't worry, we can count on it. Well . . . that or suicide."

Devorah shook her head. "Don't you understand that Jonathan would *never* have missed the chance to get inside? *And* that Chamber 11 student avoided me today as if she was guilty of something Jonathan-related."

"Don't *ever* call her that. Seven is the absolute limit. And while you're at it, call *him* 'The Other'."

Akiva paced the office. "You do realize that if that woman is harboring Professor Bezalel's assailant *and de-tohuing-v'bohuing* Fifth Dimensional psychopaths, then we've reached an all-time low."

Devorah nodded and shrugged her shoulders in complete dejection. "We have. Today in the vault, I sensed that we're missing some *EPIC* window of opportunity. *We're* the ones being cut off . . ."

Ezra tapped nervously on his desk. "It's Professor Bezalel. *Daniel.* He's the key, and we've failed him."

Devorah started trembling and then shot up out of her seat. *"There's an Avarshina coming into the school building!"*

Akiva and Ezra both called out, *"What!"* and Ezra went on, *"is an Avarshina?"*

Akiva shouted excitedly, "Our legendary phoenix," as he ran toward the window.

Ezra immediately looked out the window too. "You mean the bird that turns into a fireball and is reborn from its ashes?? I didn't think they existed."

"The phoenix is a myth, but an Avarshina isn't."

Ezra searched the sky in every direction but didn't see a thing. When he glanced down, he saw his Great Aunt Esther struggling up the steps that led to his office. *Really bad timing.* He had totally forgotten . . . she had wanted to come by early this morning, something about losing a button in one of the classrooms when she substituted for Daniel.

Devorah rushed to the window and pointed straight at Ezra's Aunt. "*That's her! Mrs. Epstein!* Wow! I haven't seen her since sixth grade. I *never* knew. But, then of course none of us could have known. She only substituted in elementary school—*before* we entered the Chambers."

Ezra felt like his mind was reeling. *Great Aunt Esther, an Avarshina??!!*

"Don't you SEE? This makes so much sense! She's a holocaust survivor, right? Risen from the ashes. And your great grandfather—her father—he must have passed the Avarshina's gift to her. He was by far the most advanced Fifth Dimensional Luminary of his generation—"

"He was a *Mekubal*—a Kabbalah master. No one ever called them Fifth Dimensional Luminaries back in those days," Ezra said distractedly while focusing on his Great Aunt.

Akiva looked spellbound. *"Beautiful!!"*

Devorah added, "She's so glorious and majestic—more vividly luminous than I ever imagined."

Ezra couldn't fathom it. He saw only his great-aunt shuffling up the steps in her orthopedic shoes, gripping the handrail like her life depended on it, and now after the fourth step she had stopped completely to catch her breath. *Come on, come on—only two more,* he coaxed her on in his mind. Then he turned around and frantically asked, "What can she do? Put me in the picture here! What's it all mean? I can't *believe* she never told me!"

Akiva turned around and grabbed Principal Oholiov's shoulders excitedly. "That's because she doesn't even know! But, this is what we've been waiting for.

PLAYING WITH FIRE

This is the *BIG* guns! An Avarshina has one of the highest levels of selflessness. That's how it earned its gift of self-regeneration going on . . . 4,121 years now. It was a blessing from Noah himself—the Avarshina would hide in the hold of the Ark because she didn't want to trouble Noah to feed her—"

"But what's important is that they can partially *share* their gift with living creations *similar* to themselves." Devorah pointed out ecstatically.

When Principal Oholiov still didn't change his expression, Akiva shouted out happily, "*The Avarshina can resuscitate any of the 36!*"

Devorah was thrilled. "We have to take her *right now* to Professor Bezalel!"

Ezra shook his head and threw his hands up in the air. "Hold on! *Hold on . . . She's been to him!* She's been making regular hospital visits."

Devorah's face became entirely crestfallen. "Really? How often?"

"I don't know . . . I think she was there maybe twice or three times."

Akiva rubbed his forehead. "So, that's how many times she's resuscitated him *already.*" He turned to Devorah. "How many times can it work?"

A loud and slow knock was heard at the door and Ezra quickly whispered. "Believe it or not, she's coming to look for a button she lost in one of the classrooms."

Devorah shook her head and whispered back. "No. She's looking for something else . . ."

Ezra called out in the most natural voice he could muster, "Come in."

Great Aunt Esther surveyed the office with her large triple-magnification eyeglasses and asked, "Am I interrruptink sometink?"

"No. No. Of course not. I'm so glad to see you."

Devorah quickly brought her a tall glass of cold water. "Why don't you sit down and rest a minute."

Great Aunt Esther waved her hand. "No. No. Zhen it vill only be zhat much harder to get up again," she said as she slowly pulled a small white handkerchief out of her breast pocket while straining her eyes to see what she was doing. "Zhis is vat I lost. Zhere isn't anoter vone like it." She carefully unwrapped the handkerchief with unsteady hands and exposed its contents for everyone's inspection. Inside was a medium sized gold button that was shaped like a rose.

Everyone was trying their best to look especially interested.

The Avarshina was watching the burnished girl of copper. She was afire, but she wasn't an Avarshina. She had beautiful wings of flight, but she still wasn't an Avarshina. She was sending out flares everywhere to heal Bezalel, the pillar of fire. That wasn't hers to fulfill, she wasn't an Avarshina. Why wasn't she guarding the golden nest of the *Yessod*? The Avarshina had wanted to draw strength from the spot where the unique child had arisen—the child that would bring back the Shamir. Now the Avarshina understood that the unique child needed to be protected or it would end up on a sacrificial pyre—incinerated by a blaze of misdirected passion by its own guardian.

"I'd be more than happy to help you look for it. Which classroom did you lose it in?" Devorah asked as she put her hand on Great Aunt Esther's arm and then withdrew it in alarm. *The Avarshina was also protecting whoever destroyed Professor Bezalel!*

PLAYING WITH FIRE

Great Aunt Esther became adamant and insisted that Ezra should be the only one to follow her into the classroom. Devorah and Akiva were left in Principal Oholiov's office, totally speechless. They didn't have to read each other's minds to know what they were both thinking. Akiva looked at Devorah and his heart sank. She was fighting back tears, and he felt that he could envision exactly how she must have looked as a beautiful little girl.

"I don't understand. Why are the Avarshina and that Chamber 12 girl both trying to protect whoever tried to destroy Professor Bezalel? Aren't WE supposed to be the good guys!"

Akiva lowered his head. "We are. We're just not the good *enough* guys."

"We're losing this 9th of Av! And we don't even know to who or what or why!"

Akiva had his adage ready. "As long as the candle is still burning, there's still time for us to fix . . . our mistakes. Devorah, one of us or both of us is making a huge one."

Devorah grabbed her head and asked, "What do you think is blinding us?"

"I don't know. But it's OK. It's OK if we fall. We just have to know how to get back up again."

As improbable as it was, Ezra actually found the button, and then he dutifully walked his great-aunt home. The two-minute walk took ten. He couldn't help noticing that her health had severely deteriorated lately. The Old City was no place for someone her age. The uneven cobblestone alleyways were a major safety hazard, and everywhere you turned were unsteady and insecure steps leading up or down. Getting her a wheelchair was just as impractical. Why couldn't she listen to reason and abandon that one-bedroom apartment of hers? Ezra sighed. He had always thought she was just plain obstinate. But where else could she possibly live? Ezra took in the view all around him as he patiently waited for her to take another step. *The Eternal City. The Timeless City of Jerusalem.* It might be the most impractical place on earth for Great-aunt Esther, but it was the only place in the world for an Avarshina.

CHAPTER 8

Freaks of Nature

A TIME TO CRY AND A TIME TO LAUGH

"I'm going out of my mind with him climbing the walls."

"This is only his first day being grounded. What are you talking about?"

"Jessie, he's been grounded this whole summer! Because we as parents failed to provide him with a viable alternative after the Chambers were cancelled! We need to send him to soccer camp!"

"*NOW?* Of all times? When he's grounded? Just give him a reward instead of a punishment? Absolutely *not.*"

"You don't get it, do you? It's precisely *because* he has absolutely nothing to do that he's developing negative behavior traits! Can't you SEE it?!"

Jessie could see it, but Soccer Camp would only help it along in his opinion. "Okay, after he finishes his punishment, we'll see . . ."

"What?"

"We'll see . . . about that camp . . ." Jessie mumbled 'soccer' to himself, but it was barely audible.

Aaron waited until both the Davidsons' voices trailed out of the courtyard before leaving the guest room.

He then walked briskly into Elisha's room, rubbing his hands together.

"I'm expectin' an easy takeoff and landin' today!" he said loudly enough to distract Elisha from his Flightpilot game. "Come on. Let's get in there before your badge of selflessness disappears. I've got a good feelin' that this time you're gonna come back with all the answers."

"Did you hear that I'm grounded?" Elisha said without taking his eyes off the game.

"Sure did! But this doesn't count."

"No. I know. But I'm going to be stuck here at home for a *whole* week!"

"Well, that's because you shoudda taken my advice."

Elisha crashed his plane and turned around to face Aaron. "*Your* advice?"

"I told you to help a blind person cross the street, and instead ya went off like you were John Wayne or somethin'."

"What? Who? And by the way, there aren't *any* streets with cars to cross around here, and you told me to help an old lady and there weren't any of those either!"

"Oh come on, what difference does it make? I just want to see for myself if you doing somethin' selfless for a change, really *can* make a difference."

Elisha didn't like that 'for a change' bit, but he couldn't help fighting back a rising sense of self-worth when he entered the rainbow field of vision and immediately found himself in the gigantic glimmering aquamarine chamber. But King Solomon wasn't there. Elisha walked quietly over the smooth icy blue looking surface and then heard strange noises coming from the massive hall behind the throne. Elisha looked straight ahead and saw that King Solomon was talking to an animal. He

FREAKS OF NATURE

was *definitely* talking to an animal, and it was the most bizarre and amazing animal Elisha had ever seen. The first thing that came to his mind was that it was a bright unicorn peacock. Well, it had the single horn and shape of a unicorn, but its long fur, or coat or whatever it was, had vivid and bright colors of turquoise blue, deep scarlet red, and lots of purple in between. But the most wondrous thing was that the fur seemed to light up and still keep its strong colors.

King Solomon turned to Elisha. "She is beautiful, is she not?"

Elisha certainly thought so, but was overwhelmingly curious to know what *she* was.

King Solomon sensed his wonder. "Yes, it is quite a shame that you do not have any in your period. The *Tahash* are only around during Tabernacle or Temple building times." The King moved alongside the beautiful animal and started petting the long, luminous, colorful fur.

Elisha finally found his voice and asked, "Can I touch her too?"

"Of course you may," answered the King. "However, this particular *Tahash* is quite upset at the moment."

The King continued his conversation with the colorful unicorn while Elisha started stroking its fur. It felt like silk, and he couldn't stop looking at how the bright colorful strands were lighting up over his hands.

King Solomon sighed and explained to Elisha, "We once used the skin of the *Tahash* as a covering for the Tabernacle, but now we use it for making the Temple's sanctuary partition."

Elisha cringed at the thought. This was too beautiful of an animal to *kill*.

The King immediately sensed his thoughts again.

"Fear not, my son, this lovely creature is not killed for her skin, but she does shed it every three years and leaves us with the most spectacular material that exists in the Eighth Kingdom. The problem is that my own storehouses are already overstocked and we simply do not need anymore. I would send her back with you, but alas, even if she *could* make it back alive, she would only find herself in animal laboratory testing."

Elisha realized that the King was probably right. He continued to listen quietly to the curiously strange sounds of the *Tahash* conversation while petting every side of the spectacular animal in complete wonder. He was running his hands over the ivory-smooth, colorful horn when the King said something very abrupt which finished his *Tahash* talk. He then turned to Elisha with beaming eyes and a kind smile.

"I have brought an absolutely wonderful and special surprise for you today: A little selflessness celebration, if you will."

Elisha couldn't imagine what could be more wonderful than seeing and petting a *Tahash*. But his eyes carefully followed King Solomon's every step as he walked over to a triangular diamond table and picked up something spongy-looking that was laid out on a purple satin cloth. When the King came closer, Elisha could see that the something seemed to be very thick, shimmering, sandy-colored cotton candy. King Solomon was handling it as if it was the most precious substance on earth.

"I want you to have a taste of this."

Elisha thought it was weird, but he still stretched out his hand to take some of the mysterious wispy stuff when King Solomon pulled it back and said,

"Wait. Not yet. First, what is your favorite ice

FREAKS OF NATURE 159

cream?"

That was easy. "Cookies and cream."

King Solomon said, "Yes. A very good Benjamin and Jeremiah flavor."

Again, Elisha was astounded at how the King seemed to know *everything*.

The King continued with his instructions: "Good. Now, think of that and *then* taste this."

Elisha did, and it was amazing. The thick cotton tasted exactly like cookies-and-cream ice cream, and the texture was the same too. King Solomon reached out and took a tuft for himself.

"Do not mind me, but I am going to go with filet mignon with a cabernet and ground peppercorn sauce." The King made a blessing and delicately put the small piece in his mouth and slowly savored it. "Perfection." Then he motioned to Elisha, "One more, and make it a good one."

Elisha thought carefully. Regular chocolate, or white? Caramel, or a giant peanut butter cup with marshmallow? He decided to make a combo of everything, and it was the best thing he had ever tasted in his whole life.

The King didn't take a second bit for himself. He looked at it longingly and said, "I better not. The High Priest will have my head if he found out that I took some of his precious manna. There's only one omer left in the jar."

Elisha almost choked. He couldn't believe his ears. He had just tasted *manna!* It was amazing! And he was having such a good time that he couldn't understand why his watch had just beeped, signaling that ten minutes had already passed. Had he just wasted all his precious time again? He was supposed to come back with all the answers this time, now that he had his selflessness injury. Didn't the King realize he hadn't taught him anything? He apparently did, because he started speaking at a slightly faster pace, and now Elisha didn't dare to interrupt him.

"Yes, now it is time for our little experiment." He wrapped some of the manna in a cloth, then cut a beautiful lock of *Tahash* hair and put it in another cloth. He handed them both to Elisha and then said with a very serious face, "I do need to verify if items of antiquity that are *not* man-made can make it back into your world, my dear Elisha. It is paramount for the task we have at hand. One must always remember our goal. The 9th of Av, yes? And there is really very little time left in the illusion of time before we are there."

Elisha thought that was strange considering he already had the *Choshen* stone, although maybe that was man-made. He ventured to ask, "King Solomon, what about the *Choshen* stone?"

"Well, my dear boy, I suppose you would call that combo-made, and of course, the Shamir took part in forming the stone. No *thing* with a truly Divine essence can *ever* be physically destroyed once it has made contact with a Shamir. However, it is only the Shamir that can preserve its *Divine* essence."

King Solomon looked deep into Elisha's eyes and asked, "Now does the *Yessod* understand the importance of the *Shamir*?"

Elisha guiltily shook his head "no."

"Pardon me, I was asking the *Yessod*," said the King as he broke his stare and led Elisha straight to the Ispaklaria's shadow.

Elisha was even more confused. *Aren't I the Yessod?* And there was that weird question about a Shamir again.

FREAKS OF NATURE 161

Every time he had seen Rav Kadosh he had asked him about it too. But when he thought of Aaron waiting for him, he was practically bursting with excitement. He couldn't wait to show him what he had. But the minute Elisha touched the Ispaklaria's shadow, something didn't feel quite right about the cloths in his hand. He practically smashed into Aaron's reflection while quickly opening the cloth in his left hand. The 'whole' Aaron bumped right into him, and at the same moment he saw that the beautiful crystalline manna was now a pile of maggot worms and *stank!* Elisha threw the cloth down in disgust, and the worms lay on the floor, crawling over each other in a pile. It was gross. And by then Elisha could tell that something was moving in the other cloth. He quickly tossed it into Aaron's hands like a hot potato, just in time to see a group of large black and red hairy spiders starting to crawl out of the cloth. Elisha practically hurtled into the hallway and started to uncontrollably jump around while swatting at every part of his body. He'd had a spider phobia for as long as he could remember. He could hear Aaron stamping on the floor. *Good, hopefully he's killing them all.*

Aaron was doing exactly that, except that one of the spiders had suddenly crawled up his arm, and when it did, he was very surprised to see it transform into the strangest thing—a glowing turquoise-blue kind of hair. He called after Elisha, *"Will you get back in here!* What's the matter with you?! They're *only* spiders!" Aaron glanced at the glowing hair, "Aren't they??"

Elisha shouted out from the hallway while still checking every part of his body. "Are they all dead?"

"Well, yes."

Elisha was torn. "Are you sure that *every single one*

of them is dead?"

"*Yes*, so get back in here, NOW."

But then Elisha heard another foot stomp. It was enough to make him hesitate. "I thought you said they were *all* dead?"

"Well, now they *are!*" Aaron shouted back.

Elisha cautiously came into the room while searching all over it and sighed, "That was a really *bad* experiment."

Aaron asked, "You want to tell me now why you brought back a spider's nest and a pile of maggots? Or was that part of the experiment?"

Elisha saw that Aaron was holding the beautiful strand of *Tahash* hair.

"Hey, you've got it! How did you get it?"

Aaron rolled the strand between his fingers, "This? What is this? One of the spiders crawled on my hand and then turned into whatever this is . . ."

Elisha's voice turned urgent. "Aaron, grab the maggots with your hand."

Aaron looked at Elisha with sheer disgust. "You're runnin' a mile from these cute furry spiders and you want me to touch a pile of maggots. Forget it." He looked down at the slithering pile and shuddered, "Nope. Sorry, I've got a worm thing."

"Aaron, you've got to *try,* because believe it or not, that was actually *manna* when I left King Solomon."

Aaron took a deep breath and scooped up the pile of maggots with his bare hand. They instantly transformed into the fluffy crystalline manna. Elisha was about to have Aaron do the taste test, but his stomach lurched. Neither one of them would ever be able to put it near their mouths after having seen it as a pile of worms. But he still grabbed for it, only to find himself holding the pile of maggots again. Elisha shook his hand violently and the maggots went flying, scattering all across his room.

"Good job!" Aaron said sarcastically.

Elisha looked at the damage and sheepishly suggested, "Maybe we can sweep them all back up again into a pile?"

Aaron shoved Elisha back into the hallway. There were three thick spiders coming off the ceiling right over Elisha's head. Elisha left the room swatting at the air in every direction while shouting to Aaron to grab a hold of them. After what felt like five long minutes, Aaron came into the hallway with a handful of colorful *Tahash* hairs. He smiled at Elisha and held his hand out to him. "You want some?"

Elisha dashed at full speed to the other end of the house while Aaron called over his shoulder, "You'll have to fill me in later or I'll be late for work."

Elisha trailed after him. There was *no way in the world* he was going to take the risk of going back into his tarantula-infested room. He headed to the kitchen carrying a nagging thought that King Solomon should have told him to give the things to Aaron in the first place. Hadn't he known that? It wasn't Elisha's fault. But come to think of it, Elisha didn't even know *why* they were doing the experiment.

Elisha was about to open the fridge when he saw a big note on it from his mother. It was a shopping list that he needed to get from the grocery store. He was allowed out for that. He happily went to do the chore. It was a lot safer *out* there.

Jonathan couldn't help feeling slightly anxious as he walked into Dr. Brody's office. He still had a tinge of *tohu v'bohu* trauma and just the fleeting thought of a relapse completely unnerved him. He became even more apprehensive when Dr. Brody seemed happy to see him. Jonathan was told to 'relax' in the chair, as if that was humanly possible with the amount of caffeine in his system. He was also too burnt out to read Dr. Brody's mind, so he ended up enduring three excruciating minutes of evasive garble until Dr. Brody finally got to the point.

"And that's why I've come to the conclusion, Jonathan, that you most likely *were* a human guinea pig in a laboratory experiment by some extremely dangerous and twisted minds."

Jonathan glowered. Those words were said so enthusiastically, they could have been announcing the winner of a 100-million-dollar lottery. A bitter taste started rising in his mouth, especially when Dr. Brody excitedly boasted of how he had done his research on Professor Bezalel's theories and on practical Kabbalah and how he had figured it *all* out and poor, *poor* Jonathan was very likely, indeed a *victim*.

Well, he had definitely found the tip of the iceberg, and Jonathan did *not* want him there. Now he'd have to resort to some skillful manipulation in order to keep Dr. Brody in line. Jonathan lowered his head and acted sincerely appreciative and forever thankful that Dr. Brody *believed* him now.

"So now you *can* understand why Chamber Seven is *so* important. It's when Professor Bezalel wiped away all of my Chamber memories!"

"*Of course* I understand, Jonathan. We absolutely need to record that session in particular. But remember that whatever the date is, it's vital for you to *name* Professor Bezalel, or we won't have anything to work with. You have a rather bad habit of always referring to him as

FREAKS OF NATURE 165

the 'Arranger of Letters' or some another pseudonym, and we need his name to be recorded. Is that understood?"

Jonathan reached for his cellphone, set it up for voice recording, and hit the red button. Dr. Brody realized that there were still trust issues. But other than that, he was sure that he had made tremendous progress with the patient, and now they were both working *together.*

At the end of the session Jonathan was thoroughly disgusted. Dr. Brody had given him a synopsis of his Chamber lessons, and it seemed to only focus on different levels of consciousness. Dr. Brody, on the other hand, was simply thrilled thinking that he had just fortified Jonathan's legal arsenal.

"This is pure insanity," Dr. Brody chortled excitedly. "Do you know that you talked about three more types of consciousness, not just verbal and nonverbal?" Dr. Brody looked at his notebook. "There was Continuous Consciousness, Scintillating Consciousness and Illuminating Consciousness." Dr. Brody was sure that he had discovered a consciousness laboratory of massive proportions and was smiling so smugly that Jonathan couldn't wait to deflate him and his medieval profession.

"And uh, Dr. Brody, there's also Unity Directing Consciousness, Palpable Consciousness, Enduring Consciousness, Transcendental Influx Consciousness, Apparitive, Glowing, Glaring, Hidden, Pure Consciousness and twenty more."

Dr. Brody was delighted, but Jonathan was looking at his pompous face and thinking that the man was senile. Jonathan had transcribed every session, so he knew exactly how many times he had brought it up.

"Don't you remember how many times I said that there are 32 paths of wisdom? I recall saying that at least seven times."

Dr. Brody instantly became defensive. "And I'm supposed to deduce from that that these 32 paths of wisdom are different states of consciousness?"

Jonathan tried his best not to roll his eyes. "Hmm ... Dr. Brody, we've only established that the Chambers programs are one big summer camp for experimental mind control. They're not taking place in some sunny pine tree forest on a lake, but in a pitch-black dimensionless vault that's entirely thought-bound. Hmm ... So, let's see. What else in the world would they be? 32 popsicle-stick projects?"

Dr. Brody couldn't help feeling resentful. Here he was trying to be professionally helpful, and Jonathan was still trying to insult his intelligence. But now the case was too important to relinquish.

Jonathan slouched and frowned. The main thing was that this session was another *miss*—no revelatory Chamber Seven lessons and nothing about accessing the Foundation Vault. He'd have to come back, and now he *hated* this modern monstrosity of an office more than ever. The panoramic windows were a disaster. Each glass pane had a separate reflection, and each reflection was obscured by a dark shadowy form. It was *totally impossible* to ignore it.

Elisha made a wild dive to save half his popsicle as it slid off its stick and ended up smashing one of his grocery bags onto the Jerusalem stone alleyway. He was opening the bag to check if anything had broken when he heard someone breathing out heavily in the creepiest voice:

"I'm starving. I'm starving."

FREAKS OF NATURE 167

Elisha turned quickly around, but there was no one in sight.

"I'm *starving*, I'm STARVING."

It sounded like the voice was following him. Elisha stopped and searched all his surrounding space for the voice. Nothing. The pathway was deserted. Elisha froze. Were Avshalom's brother and his friends playing a prank on him?

"I'm going to die of starvation, you pig-colored person."

Elisha knew now without a doubt where the nasty voice was coming from. It was from a small-sized, brown and white, scraggly-looking dog straight across the alleyway. Elisha made eye contact with it and heard the voice again.

"That's right, little humabing, I'm over here. So now look at my cute doggy face, say awww and feed me."

It *was* the dog. And it wasn't cute. Without understanding how or why it seemed so natural, Elisha answered. He was just surprised that he could make such weird noises come out of his throat as he told the dog, "Come here."

A spasm of shock went through the dog's body as it cocked its head and pricked its ears up high. "What are you, some kind of freak?" it yowled, completely stunned.

Elisha couldn't help smiling ear to ear at his new 'gift of wisdom,' and he growled and barked back with gusto, "You should be nice to someone who's about to feed you!"

The dog ran toward Elisha and pitter-pattered close to his heels with his tail wagging furiously. "Okidoggi, you're so cute I could just blubber your face with my spit, and by the way, I *don't* eat that disgusting dog food with the stupid shapes that stinks like last week's garbage."

Elisha's face scrunched up. Having never spoken to a dog before in his life, he couldn't have known any better, but *still* this somehow wasn't the personality he expected a dog would have. Or maybe it was just *this* dog.

"I do like pink blimps. I can smell them in your bag,"

Elisha watched as the dog sniffed at the shopping bags, and Elisha growled back low and softly, "They're called *hot dogs*."

Aaron was surprised to see Elisha in the courtyard talking to a dog when he got back.

"What in the world are you doin'?"

"I'm talking to the dog."

"Well, I could tell, like you were growlin' and barkin' or somethin'. What *is* the matter with you?"

"This is Mushball. He followed me back from the grocery store."

Aaron looked around the courtyard. "Aren't you breakin' the groundin' rules? And you know your father hates dogs. You're just gonna get yourself into more trouble!"

"No. You don't understand. I've been really *talking* to him all afternoon. That's how I know his name, Mushball. He's seven years old, and by the way, a dog's year is the same as ours, not seven, they just age quicker and die faster. Anyways, he was lost, and I even found his family. They're coming to pick him up later."

Aaron went over to pet the dog. "*Awww*, cute little Mushball doggie."

"He's not."

"What?"

"He's not cute *at all*. Believe me, I got to know him."

Mushball growled at Elisha. "I'm dying of thirst from the pink blimps. *Water! Water!* Stop making humabing noises and bring me water!" the dog whined and panted.

Aaron stood by and heard all sorts of strange noises coming out of Elisha's throat and mouth as he answered something to the dog. Aaron blinked. *Right. Nothing unusual going on here . . .* He stared at the dog and then clapped his hands. "Alright then! Why don't we clean up the poor mutt, so that he doesn't go home lookin' so awful."

Elisha looked straight at Aaron and smiled. "Not me, but I'll watch."

Aaron was good with dogs; he took out the hose and shampoo. But even after all the grooming Mushball still looked scraggly, but at least clean scraggly. After shaking off the excess water, Mushball ran up to Elisha and put his wet paws on Elisha's legs and asked,

"Is the big guy a humabing?"

Elisha was slow to respond, "As opposed to *what?*"

Mushball quickly answered, "How about *not a* humabing."

Elisha raised an eyebrow. He *had* to understand this business; maybe, just maybe, Mushball could let him in on some of Aaron's well-kept secrets. Aaron had turned on the hose again and was busy cleaning up the soapy courtyard and watering the plants. He was also taking side glances at Elisha and apparently getting a kick out of his dog talk. So it made him feel a bit guilty when he asked Mushball, "What's different about him?"

Mushball shook his body again and answered, "You mean you didn't *smell* him? Go ahead and smell him, *you'll* see for yourself."

"I'm *not* going to smell him. So just tell me."

"Okkidoggi, he's unbiteable."

Great, thought Elisha, that's what you get when you talk to a stupid dog.

The dog growled sharply, "Don't you dare disrespect dog tradition!! There are only 36 non-biteables on the face of the Eighth Kingdom, and your friend is one of them. But he's also something else. A combo—don't know what. Maybe if I chew on his shoe I'll figure it out."

Elisha was sick of Mushball already. "*No*. How about you just go sit, roll over or play dead instead?"

Mushball started snarling loudly at Elisha and then bared all his teeth. "I could bite a chunk out of *you* without any problem."

Aaron turned off the water and shouted over all the noise. "HEY! What's goin' on? What's he getting' all crazy about?!"

"You don't want to know."

Aaron coiled up the hose and headed out of the courtyard.

"Where are you going?" Elisha asked.

Aaron just winked and said, "Well, you made me feel left out, so I'm goin'."

He had barely left the courtyard when Elisha's father walked stiffly into it and nodded a hello.

Elisha thankfully wasn't having a dog conversation. But his father still looked at him strangely and then walked straight into the kitchen.

"Tamar, Elisha is in the courtyard with a *dog*."

"I know."

"But he's grounded."

"Relax. He didn't break any rules."

FREAKS OF NATURE 171

"Then where did he get the dog from?"

"It found him. And he found the owners. So he's actually in the midst of doing a good deed."

"But it's going to be dark soon. Certainly there should be some limitations on outdoor time or how much fun he gets to have."

"Actually, he would have been in the house hours ago already if it didn't take you so long to come home from work."

"What?"

"Well, he apparently found monster-sized spiders in his room this morning, and you know how he is about them, and don't look at me like that! You know I can't do it either."

Jessie felt his aggravation rising. Here he had barely gotten home and already he had something distasteful to take care of. He didn't waste any time with his task. He called from the front door, "Elisha, get in here."

Elisha left Mushball and went inside.

"Okay now do you want to tell me where these 'monster' spiders of yours are?"

Elisha could have killed himself. He shouldn't have told his mother about them. The last thing he needed was his 'Terminator' father to be involved. And Aaron had picked a lousy time to disappear. He tried to get out of it.

"I don't know. They're probably all gone now."

"If they were ever here to begin with."

"No, Dad, really you should have seen them. They were huge, and poisonous too." Actually Elisha wasn't even sure if there *were* any left. Refusing to go into his room had just been a kind of safety precaution. Elisha followed his father only up to the doorway, and he was surprised to know immediately. There were three. One was under his bed, another was hiding under a pile of clothes on the floor in the middle of his room, and a third was behind his closet. He could *hear* their silent thinking and also somehow knew that they weren't poisonous either. Their language was thick and low and slow. The one under his bed was feeling comfortably dark and cool, while the one under his dirty clothes was feeling soft and safe. Elisha immediately thought of *Charlotte's Web* but blocked it out. He *hated* that book! Nothing anyone could ever say or write would change things. Spiders *were creepy and disgusting,* and now he also knew they couldn't spell, but he still tuned into their thoughts. The one behind his closet was thinking differently. It was a female spider and Elisha understood that she was about to give birth. The thought practically paralyzed his mind with fear. Why hadn't he done this before when Aaron was around to take care of them!

His father broke his silent communications and announced, "Well, I don't see a thing."

Elisha blurted out, "There's one under my bed, one behind the closet and one under that pile of clothes." And Elisha pointed to each spot quickly. Elisha's father raised his eyebrows and headed for the pile of clothes first, when Elisha suddenly shouted from the doorway, "Stop!"

"What is it now?"

"I, I don't want you to kill them."

Mr. Davidson's face seemed entirely shocked when he turned to Elisha and said, *"What?"*

Elisha knew he couldn't destroy them just because he was scared to death of them for no reason, especially since Aaron could transform them when he got back. "I have an idea, I'll get a plastic container and we'll get them to crawl inside it, and then you can put them into

FREAKS OF NATURE 173

a forest or something."

"That's noble of you, Elisha," his father said with a stunned expression.

Elisha ran out and came back quickly with a large plastic container. The spiders were still in their low monotone thoughts. Elisha knew that he didn't need to make a sound; instead he allowed his brain to vibrate slowly and deliberately in spider language. "Sorry, you cannot be in this room. Come out now and no one will get hurt. Crawl out of your hiding places and into the box I'm going to put on the floor. We'll take good care of you."

A chorus of vibrations entered Elisha's mind. Elisha could tell they were all stiffening their legs and their hairy bodies were bristling in fear.

"We cannot. We are more scared of you than you are of us."

Elisha was shocked. *Wow,* they really did think that! Elisha braved himself to set down the plastic container in the middle of his floor and then ran back to the doorway and vibrated his message again. "Do not be scared. It is good. I promise." Elisha covered his eyes and watched through just a crack of his hands as the spiders started to crawl out of their hiding places.

The pregnant spider came out first, and then the other two.

Mr. Davidson was immediately horrified. With good speed and skill he stepped on all three of them as quickly as he could while Elisha shouted out,

"*Dad! STOP!*"

But it was too late.

His father looked at him incredulous.

"*Elisha. What's gotten into you!* Those *were* the biggest spiders *I've ever* seen!! You don't take chances with things that *big*. They *were* probably poisonous too!"

Elisha swallowed hard. "They weren't! You killed them! You *killed them!!* And one . . . and one of them was even *pregnant*."

"Get in here," Mr. Davidson demanded.

"No. I'm not going back into my room now. It's, it's full of spider blood." And with that Elisha rushed out of the house while Mr. Davidson just continued to shake his head in complete exasperation.

Elisha ran back to the courtyard feeling absolutely horrible about himself only to find Gila and Shira singing an annoying song to Mushball.

"Say bark bark to the sweet doggie," Gila urged Shira. "Bark, Bark, the doggie goes bark bark and woof woof. Woof woof, bark, bark."

Mushball cocked his head and in a sharp yelp said, "I *like* her. She's *very* biteable."

Elisha didn't dare speak 'dog' in front of Gila but instantly became alarmed.

"Gila. Maybe you shouldn't get too close to him. You know, I really don't know if he bites or not."

Gila snorted and let Shira whop Mushball on the head.

"If he didn't bite *you* all this time, he's not going to bite *us!*"

Mushball snarled, "The little one has *very* chewy sweet-looking arms."

"That's it!" Elisha picked Mushball up. "You and Shira need to wait inside."

"NO way. The owners are coming in five minutes, *right?* I know. Your mother said so. And we want to be *here* for the reunion." She shot a crooked smile at Elisha just as two elderly people entered the courtyard.

Elisha watched as Mushball shot off like a bullet and bounded right into an old woman's hands. Elisha looked up at Mushball's owners. They looked . . . kind of like Mushball. The woman was crying.

"My baby, my poopkiepoo, my sweet Mushballaroonie boobiebaby! Thank God you're alive!" Mushball whimpered sadly and she hugged him tighter to her breast. "My poor pumpkinoopie don't cry, you're back with mommykins now." She started kissing Mushball everywhere and Mushball snorted loudly to Elisha:

"These old and dying humabings just love me."

Elisha tried not to burst out laughing. He turned around to at least share a snigger with Gila, but she was *crying!*

Then the old lady turned toward her husband and snapped harshly, "Irving. The boy," and motioned him in Elisha's direction.

The elderly man put his arm on Elisha's shoulder and walked him off to the side.

"My wife is very ill, son. This dog means the world to her."

Gila overheard and started crying even harder while the man proceeded to take out his wallet and hand Elisha 1000 shekels. Elisha's eyes almost popped out of his head when he saw the money. But he instantly handed it back. He knew that he could *never* make money off of King Solomon's wisdom, but the elderly man wouldn't hear of it.

"Sorry, son. I'm a man of my word, and that's the reward. If you don't want it, then give it to someone who does."

Elisha turned around and looked at Gila. She was whimpering uncontrollably and wiping the tears off her face. The elderly couple started walking away just as Aaron showed up and quickly gestured to Elisha with a huge smile across his face.

"Why don't you *walk* these nice," and then he mouthed the word OLD, "people back to their car. It's almost dark."

Elisha smiled back and guided the elderly couple through the alleyways and plazas back to the Old City parking lot. It was a good thing too, because it had gotten dark and the old man nearly tripped over the curb trying to get into a cab. The old lady plunked herself into the back seat and opened the window. She kissed Mushball's paw and waved it bye bye through the window in Elisha's direction. Mushball did kind of look cute to Elisha at that moment, and then he started barking loudly and furiously. Elisha cocked his head and tried to focus, but it was gone. All he could hear was barking.

Mr. Davidson went back into the kitchen and threw a large pile of paper toweling into the garbage.

Tamar barely looked at him and asked, "Did you take care of it?"

"Yes! But he still wouldn't go back into his room!"

"I wonder why . . ."

"Tamar! Go check for yourself. I went through every inch of that room and there's none left. And believe me, *I did*, because I've got to tell you I *never* saw such big spiders here, *ever!*"

Tamar shuddered. "No, thank you. I want you to get the whole house fumigated tomorrow."

"So do I."

Tamar shuddered again. "Well, can you use something else in the meantime, something organic, so we can sleep in the house tonight?"

"Yes, we'll have to and oh, here," Jessie handed Tamar a post-it note.

"Dr. Margaret Shapiro?"

"Yes. She's the best in her field."

Tamar took her husband's hand and gripped it strongly with her own. "Thanks, Jessie."

Without any warning Gila barged into the kitchen and reached for some paper toweling. "That was SO good. It was just like watching a really bad TV movie!" she said as she bumped into the door on the way out.

"You see," Tamar said, "when he has something to keep him occupied it builds his character."

Jessie eyed Elisha coming back into the house. He did look satisfied with himself for doing a good deed. But his suspicions came back full force as he watched Elisha head straight for Aaron's room. "Maybe, but then why does he hang around with *him* so much?"

Tamar wasn't in the mood to answer, *well, probably because you don't.*

Aaron was in the middle of his home exercise routine, but Elisha still reached into his pocket and started waving his money in the air. Aaron stopped counting his sit-ups and looked at him furtively.

"Where did you get that from?"

"There's a thousand shekels here," Elisha grinned excitedly. "I got it as a reward for finding Mushball."

"Whatcha gonna do with so much money, huh?" Aaron asked as he went back to his sit ups.

Elisha stared straight at Aaron. "I kind of thought

you'd take care of it for me—you know, put it wherever you put the rest of your change from King Solomon."

Aaron smiled and scruffed up Elisha's hair. "Sure can do," he winked.

Elisha smiled back. "I'm definitely going up *lots* of notches on the selflessness scale, aren't I, right?"

"Hey," Aaron warned, "don't you start gettin' full of yourself either," and he grabbed a towel and wiped his face. "And don't forget that you're *also* tutorin' me in computers. That should count for some selflessness too."

"Yeah, right," said Elisha. "I don't think turning you into a FreeCell addict really qualifies."

"I wouldn't worry about it kiddo, you're on a *roll*!"

CHAPTER 9

Dads and Demons

A TIME TO SHUN EMBRACES

Jessie Davidson couldn't shake off the bad feeling that was gnawing at him. The incident with the spiders was too bizarre. It irked him so much that as he prepared for bed, he even decided to 'share.'

"There *is* something *seriously* wrong going on with Elisha. He's *not* acting like himself and, and . . . I'm not even sure what it is. Just look at him . . . on top of the crazy nightmares, sun stroke, starting up a fight—"

"And bed wetting," Tamar added.

"And never bothering to even open any of the books I gave him. You know what he did? He actually raised his voice to me for *killing* the spiders!"

"Really? . . . That's weird."

"I know . . . I just can't put my finger on it . . ." Jessie sat down on the bed, took off his glasses and rubbed his eyes. "You know, maybe it's got something to do with that antiquated rock in his room, maybe it's got radon or something." He rubbed at his nose. "Or it's that Kohen character. I especially don't like how he's spending *so* much of his time with him . . . I mean we both know that he's—"

Tamar cut him off. "*You* were the one who said he had exceptional attributes for a role model. You said he was a real-life hero."

"I know, but I don't like the whole story anymore. Can't you see for yourself? I'm not saying he's not a good man, but come on, he's that macho, physical type of a *guy,* and just look at how that's already had a *bad* influence on him."

Tamar put a bookmark in her magazine. "Well, what do you want to do?"

"I want to get rid of that stone and then Kohen."

"But, I thought he was working out great at the library."

"The library is one thing. Having him in our house is another."

"But it gives Elisha time to give him computer lessons."

"Oh, give me a break, he barely knows the basics, Elisha is probably just teaching him that brainless Flight-pilot game of his."

"Well, I just can't agree with you. First off all, I'd much prefer Elisha spending his summer days with him than on the street." Tamar reopened her magazine. "I *told* you we should have sent him to soccer camp."

"Don't start."

"I am going to start, because I can't even believe that you would be so heartless to think of putting Aaron *back* on the street. And as for the mirror stone, you'd absolutely destroy Elisha if you took it away."

"Really, Tamar. I'm talking about the boy's mental health, and you're just talking gibberish."

"Right!" Tamar said angrily, "right, *just look* who's

DADS AND DEMONS 181

talking about his mental health. If you had listened *to me* sooner, we could have gotten him *real* professional help, but no, now we've got to wait for an appointment, and in the meantime your therapy plan is what? Oh, right, just take away the very things he cares about!"

Jessie looked at her with heightened suspicion and said in exasperation, "Oh come on, don't tell me that you buy that ridiculous story about your grandfather giving him the stone, do you?"

Tamar didn't take her eyes off her magazine and answered, "No, and yes!"

"Tamar!"

"Well my grandfather, blessed be his memory, was a very unusual man, and—"

"Tamar, *stop* this nonsense! He died before he could have even done it. *You know that as well as I do!!*" With that Jessie got off the bed and stomped out of the room.

What Tamar never told anyone, was that she had in her possession her grandfather's will. Well, it really wasn't a will; it was just a short letter that he had left to his beloved granddaughter that she had found a week after he had passed away. It was only a small piece of paper asking her to take care of a few worldly things, but it clearly said that he was leaving Elisha the mirror stone that was found in the bathroom during renovations. She had no intention of ever telling anyone about it, and she had absolutely no intention of ever questioning it. What worried her now as she fell off to sleep was how she'd be able to honor that small piece of paper?

Mr. Davidson, on the other hand, couldn't fall asleep at all and started pacing the floor. Was he the only normal and sane person in the whole house? He walked into Elisha's room and saw him fast asleep. Why did he keep the stone wrapped up like that at night! Another crazy piece of *mishegas!* He removed the blanket on the spot. And that would just be the start of it, he thought to himself triumphantly as he went back to his own bedroom.

Elisha was in a deep sleep. He was dreaming about the ocean; waves and waves were coming through the mirror stone and filling up his room. It was very relaxing and refreshing, until he felt that the water was going to come up over his head. It was going to choke him, but it couldn't. It stopped at his amulet necklace, the one he had made out of the inscribed parchment that Rav Kadosh had given him. The waves had barely touched the amulet and then the ocean went back into the mirror stone in reverse waves. It was a cool dream and not scary at all. But Elisha woke up nonetheless. And when he did, he was horrified to see that the mirror stone was uncovered. He looked frantically in every direction. Hadn't the Rav warned him that if he didn't cover up the Ispaklaria at night it would be the end of him? Where was the bloody black dinosaur snake thing that had come out the last time the Ispaklaria wasn't covered? He didn't even want to dare look under his bed or in his closet. He quickly ran to the Ispaklaria and covered it back up. Maybe his dream *was* real and Rav Kadosh's parchment had saved him? Everything would be okay, he told himself.

What Elisha didn't notice was that there were fresh tiny footprints on his floor coming from the direction of the Ispaklaria. Actually they weren't footprints at all; they were tiny bird prints.

Everything happened very quickly that next morning. His father walked into his room and went right to work. He

DADS AND DEMONS   183

untied the blanket from the stone.

"*This* again! I thought I took this off already!"

Elisha was up in a second and jumping to his feet. "Dad! What? What's going on?"

"I'm taking this mirror stone *off* the wall, *out* of your room and *out* of the house, *today*!"

Elisha became hysterical: "No, you can't, you can't, *you can't!*" He ran to his father's side and was shocked to see that his father's reflection was just as black as Josh's. How had he missed *that*? Maybe because his father only came into his room at night? His mother ran into the room the minute she heard all the commotion.

"Jessie, this is unnecessary!" she tried. But he was determined.

"This is for your own good, Elisha; you'll thank me for this one day!"

"*NO!*" Elisha cried.

His father was trying his hardest to move the stone, but once again it seemed embedded into the wall from time immemorial. Elisha's mother gently tried to move his father's hands, but . . . she had no reflection. Elisha stopped short and couldn't even breathe. How was it that Elisha never noticed *that* before? His own mother was one of the 36??!!! He was totally astounded. *It couldn't be.* But nothing would matter ever again, if his father wouldn't *stop*. Now his father was rushing purposefully out of the room, so Elisha quickly and desperately tried to convince his mother.

"Mom, I'll do anything you want *forever*, just *don't* take it. I promise, *forever!*"

His father was back a second later with a large hammer. He wasn't going to *smash it*, was he? Was he really going to destroy . . . Elisha ran to grab his hands, and he actually stopped him. But it wasn't his own strength that had done the job. His father had become frozen stiff. Elisha fell back in shock. He looked at his mother, but she hadn't even noticed. She seemed to be looking at something in the Ispaklaria and mouthing words. Elisha tried to follow her lips, but she was just mumbling. Although Tamar Davidson clearly heard herself saying, *"Someone's calling me."*

At that very second, Elisha was wondering if the Ispaklaria *should* leave the house. Nothing in the world could be worth his father being harmed or his mother acting crazy. He'd take it and break it himself. What had he done to his family? His mother was the first one to speak, as if she had read his mind.

"It's okay, Elisha. I know that Saba Gabriel meant for you to have this stone, and that means *only* good can come of it." She had barely finished speaking when Elisha's father instantly unfroze. He was in an entirely different mood, and seemed pleasantly confused.

"Tamar, how can you possibly expect me to hang a picture on this solid boulder?"

"You know, I don't even know why I asked you to," she answered in a daze. And then they both walked out of his room.

Elisha couldn't believe his eyes or ears. His mother had just *helped* him. His mother was on his side, and not only that, maybe she was one of the 36! And she didn't even know it! He started counting in his mind—Rav Kadosh, Mom, Aaron. Three out of the 36 on the whole planet just happened to be right around here? That seemed like very weighted odds. And his father was definitely *not* the warrior, black-shadow type, was he? Had he misread everything? Was the Ispaklaria malfunctioning today?

DADS AND DEMONS   185

The morning hubbub ended quickly, and both his parents and Shira all left together. Elisha was so relieved he could have shouted. And what happened next was even better. A familiar voice was calling to him from his window. Elisha turned around. It was Rav Kadosh!

"Let me in, Elisha," he called.

Elisha was thrilled.

"Rav Kadosh, I can't believe you're here! You can come in through the front door, my parents left already."

"No, no. I can only come in through the window."

Elisha was skeptical. "Can you fit through the window?" He was sure that with the decorative iron grating, he wouldn't be able to get though, but in the second that Elisha had turned around to think of some alternative plan, Rav Kadosh was already standing in the room. *Wow*, thought Elisha to himself, *how did he do that?* But suddenly there were three wild dogs trying to get through the window too. They were barking and growling fiercely. Rav Kadosh slammed the window shut and injured one of the dog's paws. It scampered away yelping, and there was blood left on the window. Elisha looked at the spot confused. He didn't think that the 36 ever did things like that. Saba Gabriel never would have. Maybe those dogs were really evil?

The Rav hummed to himself and walked straight past the Ispaklaria, and that's when Elisha again saw something strange going on with the reflections. He could *see* Rav Kadosh's reflection, but it was sort of yellowish. That was strange. Did Rav Kadosh suddenly stop being one of the 36? And didn't King Solomon tell him that yellow was a color he hoped he'd never see? The Ispaklaria was being really weird today. But Elisha didn't want to waste any time. He quickly spoke up.

"Rav Kadosh, my father almost destroyed the Ispak-laria. He wanted it out of the house. He uncovered it last night, and I think if it wasn't for the parchment amulet you gave me, I might have drowned." But something else was strange. Rav Kadosh didn't interrupt him and didn't even seem to be in a rush this time. Not only that, he even let Elisha calmly tell him the whole story.

"Well, that's precisely why I'm here, my boy. We have to move the Ispaklaria someplace safe."

"What do you mean? You mean, move it *out* of my room?"

"Yes, absolutely. You saw for yourself, your father almost destroyed it. Would that be any better?" he glared.

There was something different about Rav Kadosh's tone of voice and especially his eyes, Elisha couldn't quite say what it was, but it was the first time that he had ever felt *scared* of Rav Kadosh. Suddenly there was a knock on the door.

"Don't let anyone in!" Rav Kadosh ordered and quickly locked the door.

It was Aaron.

"Elisha, let me in."

There was more knocking.

"Come on, let me IN!" Aaron was persistent. "*Let* me in, Elisha. Let me in *now!*"

Elisha was torn. He looked back and forth at the door and at Rav Kadosh, whose expression was firm. He chose to obey the Rav and lamely answered, "I, I can't, I'm busy."

Aaron hurled himself against the door with all his strength, and the lock popped. The minute his eyes met Rav Kadosh, the Rav started squealing. It was a horrible noise that completely unnerved Elisha, but what happened

DADS AND DEMONS

next was even worse. In front of their very eyes, Rav Kadosh was changing form and shrinking into something utterly disgusting. A small black pig with red eyes and the feet of a chicken was suddenly running around the room and begging for mercy.

"Save me, save me, I am only the messenger. Spare my life."

Aaron didn't seem in the mood to be merciful. He grabbed the pig by its throat and started to take it toward the Ispaklaria. The pig demon became enraged and started squealing and laughing.

"Do what you want, but my master will be back, you've released me, and I'm NOT going back."

Aaron squeezed his fist tighter, but the little figure suddenly evaporated into red dust in his hands.

All Elisha could say was, "That wasn't Rav Kadosh, was it? I knew there was something strange about him the whole time."

"Yeah, right. That's why you didn't let me through the door!"

Elisha ignored him and said, "I should have figured it out from the start. It was my father. He uncovered the Ispaklaria last night, and that thing must have come through."

Aaron was worried. "Great!"

"Aaron, what do you think that thing was?'

"Obviously, it was a pig chicken! Come on, you think *I* know! We better go and see the real Rav K right away!"

"I *can't*. You know I'm grounded. And you heard him. He doesn't want to even look at me until the 8th of Av!"

"But I think this is a good enough reason."

"Can't you go to him? *Please!*"

Aaron looked at the red powder all over the floor. It didn't look like sparkling fairy dust, and now it was turning into smears of blood. It didn't take him too long to reach a decision. He looked at his watch.

"All right! I'm gettin' over there right now. And stay out of the room in the meantime."

Aaron found the Rav with no problem. Strangely, the building seemed deserted, and Aaron was afraid Rav Kadosh's room would be empty as well. But he was right there in his study, along with the pig chicken in a cage on his desk. Aaron didn't know quite what to say, but Rav Kadosh did.

"Well, I don't know why that boy thinks that I have nothing better to do than to chase this riffraff. I've explained to the boy more than once that I'm not allowed to leave my post, and here I am running after *this*." He pointed to the pig chicken. "Where is the Shamir? Does this look like a *Shamir* to you?"

Aaron shook his head no, though he wondered how he was supposed to know what a Shamir looked like.

Rav Kadosh seemed frustrated. He looked at Aaron head on and demanded. "So *where* is the *Shamir?*"

Aaron was confused. Why was the Rav asking him about a Shamir of all things? The thing wasn't real, was it? Wasn't it just one of those kid's legends like dragons, unicorns and fairy-god-mothers? But at least you knew what those were supposed to have looked like. There wasn't anyone on earth that knew what a Shamir looked like. So why was he even being asked?

Rav Kadosh got up from his desk and started pacing the room.

"He's *not* following instructions. I told him *not* to

DADS AND DEMONS   189

leave the Ispaklaria uncovered. I told him that he had to try and be selfless, but no. He just doesn't realize how serious all this is, and now he's very lucky to be alive."

Aaron was nodding and wondering why he was agreeing with everything Rav Kadosh was saying. The Rav also seemed surprisingly relaxed, compared to last time in Elisha's room when he had talked a mile a minute and then ran out.

Rav Kadosh leaned back in his chair and breathed in deeply.

"You know, when I discovered that the *Yessod* was a ten-year-old boy, well, I was very concerned. But then . . . it occurred to me that it had several advantages. First of all, it meant that the One and Only isn't holding our generation accountable, which is a good sign. And then there's something very special about children—they're innocent, they have a strong sense of righteousness, they believe and dream and can be very brave. On the other hand, they only look for fun, are very unpredictable, and are naturally selfish. But certainly the biggest problem is that they are terrible at *following instructions*. If you hadn't come in time, this Rav Kadosh look-alike would have killed him on the spot." The Rav seemed genuinely disturbed. "Please try and knock some sense into the boy."

Aaron was quick to promise and then ventured, "Well, what are you going to do with it?"

"What am *I* going to do with it? *I* have no idea what to do with it, but King Solomon does. Just make sure you label it DEMON so he doesn't think you bought him another laptop," he said as he pushed the cage toward Aaron. "And—WARNING—*don't* speak even *one* word to it until it's gone."

A loud woman's voice suddenly echoed throughout

the room.

"Yehuda, your breakfast is getting cold."

Rav Kadosh shouted back to the walls in a feigned sweet voice, "I'll be there in a minute, dear." And then he hurriedly scribbled out something on a parchment and handed it to Aaron. "Not a word!"

The voice now shook the room. *"I told you, your breakfast is getting cold."*

With that, Rav Kadosh jumped up as if he suddenly had to attend to a major emergency. He was so rushed that he barely managed to say, "Give this amulet to the Arranger of Letters."

Aaron was left sitting alone in the room with the pig chicken and thinking that apparently even Kabbalah masters had higher authorities to answer to. He felt clueless and just stared at the cage. Why was it that Rav Kadosh seemed to think that *he* had some idea of what was going on around here! Aaron didn't even want to guess how Rav Kadosh knew about the laptop. The pig chicken suddenly started to laugh and then cry. It was completely hideous. Now what? Should he just hang out here until the Rav finished his breakfast? Aaron heard a flapping noise coming from the ceiling and looked up. A large dark green garbage bag came floating down. He got what he had to do.

The pig chicken suddenly stared straight at Aaron with its beady little red eyes and asked, "What kind of laptop?"

Aaron almost automatically answered. He stopped himself. The ugly thing *was* tricky. He lifted the cage and then opened the bag, but just before he covered it he heard the creature laughing.

"By the way, you forgot to ask *who* the Arranger of

Letters is. But you can ask me, because I know."

Aaron looked at the small inscribed parchment he was given and immediately felt frustrated. *The darned thing was right.* He swallowed back the question and closed the bag. The thing was still talking.

"Don't worry, it's just your age. These things happen, but you should check with your doctor to make sure it's not early Alzheimer's."

Aaron had opened his mouth, but choked back his words. *That was it.* He tied the plastic handles and swung the garbage bag over his back. He also had the nasty feeling that he was cleaning up someone else's dirty laundry.

Ezra and Rebecca relocated to the hospital's visitor's lounge and sat down in the uncomfortable institutional chairs. Rebecca looked so worn out that Ezra immediately felt seized with an older-brother guilt trip. She rubbed her eyes and said,

"Ezra, I've had it with this *Paul* business already."

Me too . . .

"So what do we do now, call in an exorcist?" she said with dry sarcasm.

Ezra puffed out some air.

"And, it's not like he even *is* this *Paul*. He just has this one idyllic snapshot of himself, and that's it. I've really tried . . ."

"I know."

"I showed him *all* of his old photos—his family, schools, church, *everything,* and he doesn't recognize *anything* of his life as Paul either. I really just don't get it."

"I know. But I keep thinking that 'snapshot' memory of his must have been a *really* significant moment in his life. Of course the visual information doesn't give us much to go on. If we only had a clue as to what was going on in his *mind* at the time . . ."

"Well, if you ask me, there was nothing else. I've tried going down memory lane with him, but there's *nowhere* to go. Except that he stubbornly *insists* that we call him *Paul,* everything is still one big blank." A single tear rolled down her cheek, and she didn't even bother wiping it away.

"When do you have to decide?"

"What? About the surgery? We already did."

Ezra exhaled loudly.

"Dr. Goldman thinks he has better odds, even 42%."

Stupendous. He'll never make it. "That's encouraging. So, when?"

Rebecca stared at the wall stiff as a statue and said, "Three more days . . ." After a minute, she turned to Ezra with a tear-stained face. "What if . . . this *Paul* is here to stay?"

"It's not going to happen," Ezra assured her, but to himself he was thinking that her concern was wholly misplaced. It was Daniel who wasn't here to stay.

He shook his head and then asked. "How many times has Aunt Esther been here?"

Rebecca looked at him puzzled. "Why?"

"Because I'm asking you." Ezra replied with older brother authority.

"I don't know. Twice or maybe three times. *Why?*"

"No. Nothing. It's just that I saw her the other day and she didn't seem to be doing so well."

"Oh yeah, I know, she's getting a pacemaker put in next week."

Ezra became alarmed. "When?"

"I think on Tuesday."

"*NO! She can't! That's the same day as Daniel's surgery!*"

"So what!?"

Ezra buried his head in his hands while Rebecca shouted at him.

"Ezra. Why? *You better* tell me why!!"

"Let's go, we've got work to do," Aaron said without the slightest amount of good humor or adventurousness.

Elisha couldn't imagine what he meant, which only made Aaron angrier.

He looked up at the ceiling, "Well let me think. What looks like a pig and a chicken?"

"What, it's back?!!" Elisha said in disgust.

Aaron pointed to the garbage bag over his shoulder. "Rav K gave it back to us with his compliments."

"What are *we* supposed to do with it!?"

Aaron couldn't help enjoying the moment. He took the cage out of the garbage bag and said, "*We* aren't supposed to do anythin'. *You* on the other hand *are,* unless you want Shira to have a new one-of-a-kind designer stuffed animal in her collection."

"What do I need to *do?*"

Aaron waved his hand, "Only the usual. We've just got to send it back the way it came. And by the way while we're doin' it, FYI, it comes with a big warnin' notice that you can't talk to it or you could die."

"Really?"

"Well, maybe not die, but you definitely aren't allowed to say even *one* word to it."

Elisha and Aaron started pushing the cage through

the Ispaklaria's water*up*, but it didn't go through as easily as the shopping goods. Also, the demon kept talking away, and Elisha had to cover his mouth so he wouldn't answer it by accident. Aaron had to resort to using his full strength to shove the cage through, while Elisha watched and worried that the mirror stone would crack under the pressure of his tremendous strength. But finally, with one last Herculean effort, the cage was completely gone and Aaron removed his arms from the stone.

"I never had this much skeleton showin' before, right?" Aaron fretted as he raised his arms. One was bone to the elbow, while the other was bone until his shoulder.

Elisha tried to pretend it wasn't so bad. "Well at least you don't have fat arms."

"I *never* had fat arms."

Aaron was already heading toward the door, when Elisha reminded him.

"You've got to wait a little more, they didn't grow back yet. I mean your flesh didn't."

Aaron paced the living room not knowing what to do with himself.

"Great! I'm late already. Fine. What's today's prison schedule?"

"Those books I'm supposed to read."

Aaron said, "Good, and keep out of trouble."

"But, but what about King Solomon? You mean we're not going to get there today? We have to!"

Aaron grabbed a jacket and put his boney hands into his pants pockets

"Hey, I didn't open Pandora's Box here," he said, but as he walked out the front door he added gruffly, "All right, maybe I'll come back during the lunch break. But don't count on it."

DADS AND DEMONS

Elisha returned to his quiet room in the empty house and opened one of the books his father had given him. He didn't even understand half of the words in the first paragraph and was wondering if this qualified for child abuse, when he heard a voice.

"You were the one, you know. The one that destroyed the Arranger of Letters."

Elisha spun around quickly. There wasn't anyone in his room. He went over to the Ispaklaria and saw two red eyes looking at him from deep inside the Ispaklaria, but nothing else. Maybe the pig chicken had got encrusted too.

"You're also the only one who can fix him. Do you want me to tell you how?"

Elisha desperately wanted it to tell him how . . . .

CHAPTER 10

A SHAMIR

A TIME TO KILL AND A TIME TO HEAL

Well, what do you know, Mr. Davidson thought to himself. His little talk with Elisha had paid off. "As a matter of fact, Elisha, I'm going to be going there in an hour," he said into the phone as he continued to sort through his e-mail. "I have an appointment with the director of the hospital, and you can visit Professor Bezalel while I'm in the meeting."

They met at their car in the Old City parking lot and then drove to the hospital, while Jessie did his best to dole out what Tamar would call 'positive reinforcement.' When they arrived, Mr. Davidson walked Elisha to the door of Professor Bezalel's hospital room and left him on his own, saying, "I'll be back in half an hour to get you."

Principal Oholiov immediately noticed him and motioned for him to come into the room. Elisha walked stiffly over to the hospital bed. It seemed like Professor Bezalel's eyes were as cold as ice when he looked at him, and yet Principal Oholiov was already urging him on.

"Paul, just look at the boy closely for a minute. See if you get any kind of familiar image or even a quick flash."

A SHAMIR   197

Why was Principal Oholiov calling Professor Bezalel, Paul? Elisha wondered, as Professor Bezalel made his eyes like narrow slits and squinted in Elisha's direction. But by the looks of Professor Bezalel's empty expression, Elisha was sure the pig chicken had probably lied.

After about five seconds of staring, he spoke up.

"He does seem somewhat familiar . . . I remember. He was one of the boys you brought here a few days ago."

Elisha tried it anyway. "I used to sit in the front seat in the third row."

Professor Bezalel shook his head as if Elisha's reminder had just completely wiped out whatever he was about to say.

Ezra Oholiov knew full well that Elisha had sat in the first desk in the third row. It was the *only* reason he had picked Elisha the first time around to visit his brother-in-law. None of the students realized that this seat had any special meaning for Professor Bezalel. But Ezra knew that Daniel had reserved that seat for a student who he thought was a direct descendant of the Davidic dynasty—a potential *Yessod*. Daniel had once confided in him that he would put a student there out of instinct. And Ezra reminded himself that Jonathan Marks had once held that seat too. In Elisha's case it must have been his name Davidson—'son of David'. There was nothing more to it, he was sure. Certainly this girlish-looking boy with the big blue eyes and china-doll complexion was hardly reminiscent of the House of David. And while the boy had shown some character on his first visit, he still couldn't help looking at him with a degree of distaste. But then Daniel tilted his head to one side and spoke.

"*Wait,* I have this image, but it's fuzzy."

Principal Oholiov coaxed him on. "Good, good,

Paul, keep concentrating. What is it?"

Suddenly there was excitement in Daniel's voice and face. "This boy, this boy, this boy . . ."

He sounded like a broken record, and Elisha was getting chills, remembering what happened that day in class, but Principal Oholiov could barely contain his own enthusiasm.

"Yes, this boy, *what?*"

"Yes, this boy *is* familiar, he, he . . ."

It was obvious that Professor Bezalel was struggling hard. It was like he was trying to put some impossible jigsaw puzzle together but couldn't find the right pieces. Principal Oholiov looked like he was holding his breath. Then Professor Bezalel looked directly at Elisha's face.

"You, you, came to me on the 17th of Tammuz, you came to me with some kind of message that you couldn't understand. You brought me something, didn't you? And no, no, you came to me asking for help. You had something, and you didn't know what it was, and you needed my help. "

Elisha couldn't believe his ears! It was almost like Professor Bezalel was remembering something that *never* happened. Elisha had gotten the *Choshen* stone and *Kohen of Light* message on the 17th of Tammuz. But, as much as he wished that he could have gone to Professor Bezalel, it *never* happened.

Principal Oholiov immediately seemed to deflate; his enthusiasm vanished, and he was disappointed and upset with this strange memory. "Daniel, sorry *Paul*, no, that's *not* it. I was with you in the hospital on the 17th of Tammuz. You remember, it was when you went in for the second surgery? The problematic one? You still weren't allowed visitors. Elisha wasn't here. It must be

A SHAMIR

199

something else, try concentrating some more. Go ahead, take your time . . ."

Suddenly, Professor Bezalel gained confidence. "No, it *was* the 17th of Tammuz. That's when it *was*. It was the same day I had the surgery."

Principal Oholiov's voice was gentle but adamant. "Absolutely not!"

Elisha felt horrible. He watched as Professor Bezalel rubbed his temples like they were giving him excruciating pain.

"Wait. Wait, I know I remember him, because he came *twice*. Yes, he even came twice to see me, and the second time he wasn't alone."

Ezra had already dismissed the whole memory as ridiculous, so he wasn't interested in hearing anything else. He also didn't think it would be wise to let Daniel ramble on; he might end up saying that they met in church and that Elisha was an altar boy. But Elisha hoped he would keep going. He couldn't imagine what would be coming up next. *Who* had he been with?

Principal Oholiov looked at a far-off point out the window and shook his head in frustration. But Professor Bezalel wasn't giving up. It looked like he was going to make holes in the sides of his head with the pressure of his fingers.

"He came to me because I'm the . . . and he wasn't alone. I can't remember who he was with, but it wasn't another boy, it was a man, no, not really a man . . . he only looked like a man . . ." But it was no use. Professor Bezalel lay back exhausted on the bed.

Elisha was still looking stunned, and Principal Oholiov motioned him to leave. Elisha wished he could have stayed and told Professor Bezalel the truth, that all his finger exercises and pain were working. More than anything he wanted to tell his suffering teacher that he was actually getting his memory back, even though it was a memory of something that *never* happened.

Elisha walked slowly out of the hospital room. He had been dismissed 15 minutes early and would have to find his way back alone to the director's office. He was shaking as he walked through the corridors. How was it possible that he had *never* realized that Professor Bezalel's accident was somehow connected to everything that was going on? After all, the accident happened on the *same* day that the construction workers found the mirror stone in his house. How *stupid* could he have been? The pig chicken wasn't lying. All this time he had never put two and two together—or hadn't *wanted* to. Why hadn't King Solomon said anything about it? A chill ran through Elisha's body. Maybe somebody or something didn't *want* him to have help.

He was so quiet on the way home that even his father had asked him if anything was wrong. But Elisha couldn't get himself to answer.

It was only after he got home that he noticed it! His necklace parchment was gone! The one Rav Kadosh had given him. Fear gripped him. He wouldn't be able to tell Rav Kadosh that he had *lost* it. He had no choice but to retrace his steps, but how could he ever get back to the hospital again today?

Elisha was still searching the stone pavement near his house when he practically smashed right into Aaron.

"I'm back, but I've only got 45 minutes max. Hey what are you doin'?"

"Nothing . . ."

"Come on, what'd you lose?"

A SHAMIR 201

Elisha hesitated and then blurted out, ". . . that amulet parchment Rav Kadosh gave me."

It was the first time that Elisha had seen that grown-up face of disapproval on Aaron.

"What! How could you have let that happen?! Why weren't you more careful?"

The last thing in the world that Aaron was prepared to do was to go back to Rav Kadosh again today, and now with the missing amulet story. On the other hand, he was sure it was too serious not to take care of. "Fine. You're going to have to deal with this one yourself," he said huffily while leading Elisha to his room. "Go and get another one from the King. I'm sure he's got lots." Aaron checked his watch quickly, took a bite of his bagged sandwich and said, "Come on, you've got one chance, and if it doesn't work, I'm gonna have to head back."

Elisha felt miserable as he entered the colorful rainbow field of vision. He was sure it wouldn't work after he had messed up with the demon and now the amulet. But in less than a second he was effortlessly in the aquamarine palace, and King Solomon was seated on his spectacular throne looking straight at him.

"I would have preferred you to come alone."

Elisha looked to his left and saw that he was holding hands with IT! He shook his hand violently, but the pig chicken was still clutching onto him.

"Well, you did speak to it, did you not?" asked the King.

"I . . . I . . ."

"One word, to be precise," offered the pig chicken.

The King looked at it almost bored and said, "Yes, well, I assume you tricked him, did you not?"

The pig chicken released Elisha's hand and threw

itself onto the floor and started bawling and crying. "I helped him! I helped him! Ask him, I did!! I did!"

"And that I assume would be after you tried to kill him?" the King asked and then sighed loudly. "Very well, you may come sit on my lap, but do not get me depressed," he warned. "And the second you are finished bonding with me, it is back to Ashmodai for you."

Elisha watched incredulously as the pig chicken hopped onto King Solomon's lap and immediately turned into the sweetest, cutest pig chicken he had ever seen. The King noticed Elisha's stunned face and commented.

"These demons are just extremely attention-starved. That is how they get this way to begin with."

The pig face just smiled sweetly and started swinging its chicken feet.

"Now," said the King, "we have at least established some critical information. The *Kohen Gadol* is the *only* one that can hold onto our treasures." With that, King Solomon arose while cradling the demon in his arm and then announced in an animated voice, "It is time for you to *try* and take a Shamir with you."

Elisha's eyes lit up like rockets. The *Shamir!* He was going to take the *Shamir . . . today!!* No one had even known what a Shamir was, not even Professor Bezalel, and now he was going to be the one to find out! Rav Kadosh would be *so* happy! Elisha held his breath and waited excitedly—the Tahash and the manna had been so incredible, he could barely wait to see the Shamir. But he couldn't help feeling instantly disappointed when King Solomon picked up a very small lead-colored box and held it in his palm. He opened it right in front of Elisha's eyes, but all he could see inside was wool and some kind of grain. After another careful look, something was moving.

A SHAMIR 203

Elisha almost cringed. It was a worm. An itsy-bitsy one. And it was even ugly and deformed.

King Solomon simply said, "You would be surprised."

"Yeah," said the pig chicken.

Elisha stared into the box and saw that there was a sudden electric-blue glow to the worm, but then it disappeared. Even then, it wasn't like it was *so* amazing. Elisha asked with genuine confusion, "This is *the Shamir?*"

The pig chicken looked up at King Solomon and said, "He's being stupid."

King Solomon ignored it and closed the box and then corrected Elisha, "No. *A Shamir.*" He held the box with a concerned look and added, "And maybe not for long. While we *have* established that the *Kohen Gadol* can prevent the transfiguration of divinely made objects, I honestly do not know if anything that has a life-force in it can make it through the illusion of time when it is not the dark time." King Solomon seemed resigned and matter-of-fact. "Well, I suppose worse things have been done in the name of science." He placed the box in Elisha's right hand and sighed. "In addition, my dear descendant, judging by external appearances is a fatal flaw. *Never* belittle the power of an object because of its size."

"Yeah," the pig chicken interjected happily, and then shrank when King Solomon stared down at it.

"Like a king, the Master of the Universe creates ingenious hiding places for his most precious treasures." King Solomon stared straight into Elisha's eyes, and although he didn't say it, Elisha heard, *"like you."* "Everything is hidden, especially the Infinite One." King Solomon sat back down in his throne, but kept his eyes focused on the box. "Do not be so disappointed, my young descendant, for there is *no* thing more wondrous in this world than a freak of nature, for its very being is living proof that the Source of Sources has placed it in the Eighth Kingdom for some definite purpose." He looked deeply into Elisha's eyes and warned:

"A *Shamir* is critical. Everything will ultimately depend on you either having a *Shamir* or *not*."

"YEAH!" nodded the pig chicken.

Elisha looked at the pig chicken as he took the box. If it wasn't so cute it would have been the most annoying thing in the world. But the minute the box was in his hand, Elisha felt a sort of dread grip him. If the *Shamir* was all that powerful, maybe it could turn into a giant mutant dragon once he got home, or something even worse. He couldn't help asking, "Can it also morph into something else?"

King Solomon answered coolly, "Yes. A perfectly extinct fossilized Shamir that you could hand over to Professor Bezalel's institute as the find of the millennium . . ."

That wasn't at all what Elisha had expected, and he was astounded to hear Professor Bezalel's name. "You know him?"

"Of him," King Solomon corrected him. He turned to Elisha and focused his brilliantly kind and wise eyes on him and gently said in a low voice, "You did *not* do it to him."

It was only a few words, but Elisha felt his chest tighten. And then there were tears slowly rolling down his cheeks, and he didn't even know why. It was as if someone had discovered his deep terrible secret fear and suddenly made it disappear. The gush of relief was overwhelming.

The pig chicken pulled at King Solomon's robe and said, "But, he did do it, *he did!*"

A SHAMIR   205

King Solomon lifted the demon and told it, "Bonding time is over." A mild sonic boom shook the room, and then it was gone. The King then shifted his gaze back to Elisha.

"The Arranger of Letters did it to himself. It is the story of the moth that is attracted to the light of a flame and ends up burning itself alive. However, do not misunderstand me. I can promise you that the Chambers are not only a path of empowerment; they are truly the greatest source of power available to humankind in *this* world. But they are infinitely *dangerous*. Yes, he has made an earth shattering RE-discovery, but I am concerned that Professor Bezalel has a terrible flaw that may very well be not only his downfall, but the downfall of us all."

Elisha was drinking in every word, desperately hoping that King Solomon would tell him what it was, so that he could at least avoid it.

"He is selfless to the point of blindness. And I can only pray that he will not destroy the plan that he should have played a major role in," the King reflected. "He who moves stones will be hurt by them."

Elisha felt confused, but the King's mood became even more somber.

"My young descendant, do not think of me as an immodest man when I tell you that I had *all* the gifts of wisdom at my disposal from the Master of the Universe . . . and yet, I too failed. I too was burned."

Elisha's watch beeped, and King Solomon motioned him to head to his shadow on the wall, but he felt upset. King Solomon seemed so serious, and Elisha still had no idea what he should avoid even though it all seemed so important. Maybe the pig chicken *had* gotten him depressed. And what did he mean by so many people getting burned? He hastily asked King Solomon, "Will he ever get his memory back?"

King Solomon forced a smile. "Everything has its season, and there is a time for everything under the sun." He arose and accompanied Elisha to the shadow and instructed him, "You must try to keep your hand with the box in ultimate reality, and only when you are able to explain to the *Kohen Gadol* that he must immediately take it from your hand, may you pass it over to him."

Elisha went through the Ispaklaria with his hand outstretched behind him. He waited until Aaron wasn't only a reflection and quickly explained to him what to do. Aaron thrust his hand through the Ispaklaria and was intensely focused and ready. The box was smoothly transferred into his hand, a skeleton hand. Elisha was too embroiled in the excitement of the moment to notice. He blurted out, "It's a *Shamir*. Open it, *Open it*!!"

"*What! The Shamir!! What!!!*" Aaron lunged in place out of nervousness as his whole body seemed to guard the small box that was being grasped in his hands. And without breathing he asked incredulously, "Did you say *Shamir?*"

"Really, really!" Elisha said impatiently as he jumped excitedly at Aaron's side.

"Stand back, you're makin' me nervous," Aaron said as he carefully tried to open the small lead box. But his skeleton hand and his regular hand were shaking so much that he couldn't maneuver the little clasp to open it. He exhaled loudly and said, "Okay, *none* of this is really happenin', so let's not get so worked up."

Elisha's mouth scrunched up at hearing that one, but it apparently relaxed Aaron, because he succeeded in releasing the tiny clasp with his over-sized hands. But once the box was open, Aaron couldn't see a thing inside

A SHAMIR

it, except for some wool which he didn't think was the Shamir. He had no choice but to ask:

"Uh, what's it suppostta look like?"

Elisha answered, "It's a special worm," as he kept his distance. He was afraid of even touching the box again. So Aaron lowered it for him to take a look.

"Do you see it?"

Elisha peered into the box, but didn't see it either. "Try carefully moving the wool around a bit."

Aaron did, and then definitely noticed a tiny, dead, decayed worm. Elisha saw it too. Aaron looked at Elisha's face and asked in alarm, "Did we just kill the Shamir?"

Elisha's miserable face didn't need to answer, but he still corrected Aaron and said, "*A* Shamir."

Aaron closed up the small box. "Gee, who knew the thing was so teensy! Are you sure that's what it was?"

"Yes!" Elisha replied defensively, a little too loudly.

Aaron squeezed the small box in his hand, "I gotta tell you, I got a bad feelin' about this one. My gut's tellin' me that this was somehow really important and we blew it. You got that feelin'?"

"Yeah, because the King said that everything would ultimately depend on us having a *Shamir* or not."

That just got Aaron more upset. "Well, then why on earth did you take it today?! We've had lousy luck all day. Our battin' average has been zippo since we woke up this mornin'."

Elisha practically choked. "I . . . I forgot!! Oh no, I *forgot*!!"

Aaron put the small box in his pants pocket and absent-mindedly asked, "What?"

"To get another parchment!"

"You forgot??!! Whatta you mean, you *forgot!*"

Elisha started moving nervously around his room. "With the Shamir and everything . . ."

Aaron gave him an irate stare. "Great! Now you double blew it! Now what? I am *not* goin' back to Rav Kadosh again today. It's just *not* gonna happen."

Elisha looked gloomily at the floor. "It's okay. I'll be okay without it, I guess . . ."

"Sure, the two times the thing wasn't covered you almost got killed—once by a tornado snake and then a chicken pig—sure, it's *fine*! Who needs a powerful amulet for back-up?"

Aaron darted out of the room and started making a call.

"What are you doing?"

"I'm gettin' permission to be your parole officer."

Aaron was extremely methodical about the search. He forced Elisha to retrace his every step, including using the same hospital elevator. But it didn't help, and they eventually reached the point that Elisha had dreaded. He really didn't want to have to go into Professor Bezalel's room twice in the same day. He begged Aaron to go into the room instead. Aaron was actually happy to put Elisha out of his misery and do the dirty work himself. He was curious to take just a little peek at the legendary Temple-obsessed professor who had lost his memory on the same day the Ispaklaria surfaced.

Aaron respectfully entered the room, hoping that Professor Bezalel would be asleep so he could just perform a quick search and run; yet a part of him was wishing that he'd be awake. The first thing Aaron saw in the room was the amulet. It was being clutched in a large, bony white hand. His gaze followed the line of the body to the face. He was sleeping. Aaron was in a predicament. He could steal the amulet back, although it wouldn't really be stealing. It belonged to Elisha, and he needed it for his own protection. Or he could wake the giant skeleton and politely ask for it back. But the time he spent making up his mind did its own work. Professor Bezalel's coal-black eyes opened wide and were startled.

Aaron was apologetic. "I'm sorry, I, I, um," Aaron found himself stuck in a stammer, but Professor Bezalel finished the sentence.

"*Know* you?" Professor Bezalel was half asking and half telling him.

"No, No," Aaron repeated bashfully. "I'm just tryin' to help out a little friend of mine, and . . ."

Professor Bezalel wasn't hearing a word. He was concentrating on something else. "You're the *one!* You're the one that was here with that boy that was here this morning."

Aaron understood what Professor Bezalel was talking about—thankfully, Elisha had filled him in—but he had no idea what to do. What happened next was worse: Professor Bezalel grabbed hold of Aaron's shirt with both hands and starting begging so furiously that Aaron was frozen in shock.

"*Don't do this to me!! I'm a sick man,* my *whole life* is hanging on the *last* straws of a memory that I don't have. *Now have the decency to tell me the truth!!* You were here with that boy. You were also asking me questions. Wait! *What . . .* are you?"

Aaron was so confused his mind was spinning. He desperately wanted to help the troubled man, but how could you tell someone so sick that he was getting into something even worse for his sanity. It was too cruel, and because it was, Aaron could only continue to stare into those jet black eyes, feeling a dead emptiness and a great loss. But Professor Bezalel wasn't finished. He shouted in an unusually strong voice:

"*ANSWER ME!!*"

It was so loud that it alerted the on duty nurse, who rushed in very angry.

"*ANSWER ME!!*"

She was matter-of-fact and fast.

"*ANSWER ME!!*"

She was shooting something into Professor Bezalel's worn veins, while pointing Aaron to the door with one word, "OUT."

The amulet fell to the floor, and in a sweeping movement, Aaron grabbed it and shoved it into his pocket. The drug took effect right away, but as he strode down the hall Aaron could hear the Professor's drained and distraught voice in the background: "Stop him . . . that man . . . has the world in his pocket . . . don't let him leave . . ."

Aaron stopped short and immediately put his hand to his pocket. There were two things in it, the dead *Shamir* and the parchment amulet. But as he glanced back, Professor Bezalel was already well into a drug induced sleep. He headed out of the room and saw Elisha sitting in the waiting area, looking very worried and small. Aaron quickly took out the amulet and held it up with a huge smile.

It was only when Aaron was searching for change in his other pocket for the bus ride back that he also pulled out something else. It was the *other* parchment that Rav Kadosh had hastily given him in the morning. He told Elisha with a sarcastic voice, "OH right, lookie here, I

A SHAMIR   211

even got another one today. And this one, I was supposed to give this to . . . let me see . . . the Ranger, Terminator, no, no, it wasn't the lone ranger either, but there was an "L" in it somewhere, the Ranger of Letters. That's it! *The Arranger of Letters!*" he said sarcastically.

"So why didn't you?" Elisha asked grumpily. "Now we've got to go back there *again*!" he whined.

Aaron's face turned into a stony glare as he asked in a very low and monotone voice, "You . . . know . . . who the Arranger of Letters is*??*"

"Professor Bezalel," Elisha answered immediately, as if Aaron was brain dead. *What? He didn't know that? Everyone knew that since kindergarten at North Temple Mount.*

"And how is that his name?" Aaron asked with a rising edge to his voice.

Elisha slid into a seat and stared unhappily out the window while explaining, "It's not, you know, his real name. It's the name of the real Bezalel, I mean the first Bezalel, the one who made all the Temple things with Moses. That's what all the legends called the first Bezalel."

Aaron repeated in aggravated disbelief, "The Arranger of Letters? Come on, what kind of a weird name is that?"

"Yeah, I guess. But, it's because Professor Bezalel always taught about the Temple, so you know it became his nickname, sort of. I don't know why, but the whole school always called him that." Elisha actually thought it was a good name for him. *Professor Bezalel arranged everything. Okay maybe he didn't arrange letters, but he arranged their seats, their lessons, the Chambers . . . too bad he wasn't around now to arrange their lives.*

Aaron's frustration was festering at a deep and dangerous level. *How* was it that Rav Kadosh had *known* to give him another amulet?? And once the thought was there it started eating at him and then enraging him. He could barely speak a word on the whole bus ride home, although he certainly knew what he was going to do once he got off.

"*That's it!* We're goin' to Rav Kadosh right now!! I've had enough of being played with like I'm some kind of pawn without ever knowin' what's goin' on. He's got all the answers, he does, but he's not givin' any of them to us. Well, enough is enough! We're gonna find him, and then we're gonna stay right there until he tells us what's goin' on."

It sounded good to Elisha, and he was glad that it was an adult forcing him to go, but he still felt hesitant. "What if he doesn't want to see us? It's not the 8th of Av yet."

"Yeah, well, he might not, but I betcha he'll wanna see the *Shamir!*" And at that Aaron dashed across the Kotel plaza and bounded up the tiny staircase to Rav Kadosh's quarters two steps at a time. Elisha was left completely out of breath trying to keep up. And when they found him, he laughed.

It wasn't a nasty laugh. It was actually a very loving laugh, and because of that both Aaron and Elisha felt instantly ashamed with their accusations.

"Gentlemen. *Think* about what you're asking . . . for thousands of years all of mankind has searched for answers. *Who* doesn't want to try and understand what life and this world is *all* about?? Everything is hidden. Why do you think the *very* word 'world' in Hebrew means *hidden?* Because *everything* is. Which is *why* you are even here to begin with." Rav Kadosh stood up and quoted,

A SHAMIR   213

"After the destruction of the Temple, vision was removed from the world and given over to the insane and children."

Aaron immediately turned beet red and Rav Kadosh smiled gently.

"My dear *Kohen Gadol*, do *not* look at me offended! Can't you see that is precisely why you are such an excellent *hiding* place! It's exactly why you were both chosen for such an important mission. Who in the world would *ever* believe a barely 11 year old boy with an overactive imagination and a homeless person with a history of mental illness?"

"What are you sayin'?" Aaron asked upset and confused. "You're sayin' I *am* crazy? And because of that, I got some mission??" He stood up and pointed to his head. "Well, one of the problems with good old psycho here is that I'm apparently so crazy that I have no idea *what mission I'm on!*"

"Welcome to the Eighth Kingdom," Rav Kadosh replied. "You're *not* the only one. Every single person on this planet feels the same way. Life is trying to figure out why you're here. I do happen to know my own mission, and it's here, as the guardian of this place. What's yours?"

"That's what I'm askin' *you!! You know and you're not sharin'!!*"

"You think because I'm a Mekubal, *I know*? I can promise you that after 50 years of work, I still only get bits and pieces of the puzzle." Rav Kadosh started laughing again, but then quickly excused himself. "Sorry, the only reason I'm laughing now is because just think how absurd this is. Here you are coming to me looking for answers, and Elisha is the only one in the world in almost 3000 years to have visited King Solomon himself, the wisest man who ever lived. Now, isn't that ridiculous? Why in the world aren't you asking *him!?*"

Elisha lowered his head. He knew that Aaron was looking at him and thinking the same thing.

Rav Kadosh sighed, "Well, if you already risked coming, where is the dead Shamir?"

"See, how'd you know it was dead?" Aaron jumped in.

Rav Kadosh turned very somber. A network of wrinkles started to slowly form on his face. "Everything ultimately depends on having a *live* Shamir."

Elisha motioned Aaron to look at Rav Kadosh's face, but he didn't have to; Aaron's eyes were already focused on it.

"Gentlemen, you only need to have a little more patience. The New Moon of Av and the 'nine days of mourning' are almost upon us. Everything will become clear very, *very soon!*"

Rav Kadosh's voice became slower and thicker. "And I am *sharing* everything I can with you but at *great* cost. You understand, my boy, don't you? You think I'm being cruel limiting the times you're allowed to see me, or even the amount of time you spend with me. *No.* I'm not sure how many times you and I can be in the same room together. Your presence is aging me, or better, bringing death to me. Can you not see the effect that you are having on *all* the people who have vision that are around you?"

Elisha stood up. He wanted to run. The Rav's face seemed to be disappearing underneath folds of crumpled skin. He surely didn't want to do anything to hurt Rav Kadosh, and yet he felt the words he was saying were true.

"It's not about *me*, believe me. When I leave this world, discarding this body will be as easy as taking off my coat, and then my soul will move on. But I do have a mission, and I don't want to leave until I've completed it and have helped you figure out yours. Please give the amulet back to Professor Bezalel. I had wanted him to have it. I honestly don't know how he is involved, although he surely is, and . . ." The Rav's skull was starting to show through his forehead.

Elisha grabbed Aaron's hand and with a shaky voice he immediately promised, "*I won't come back until the 8th of Av.*"

But maybe it was even too late . . . .

Elisha didn't even try to keep up with Aaron on the way out. He was wiping his eyes and didn't want anyone to see. His body was trembling with a terrible feeling, because he couldn't pretend anymore that there wasn't something horrible happening. It had started with Professor Bezalel, then Saba Gabriel, and now it was happening to Rav Kadosh. Even the Shamir was dead. Tears were now rolling down freely from his eyes. The New Moon of Av was almost here, and *really* bad things always happened in Av! Who would be next? Aaron was the *only* person left that could help that was still okay . . . .

Aaron turned around looking for Elisha. He wasn't right behind him like he usually was, so he waited for him to catch up. He didn't need for Elisha to get any closer to see what was written all over his face. It was a look that stabbed Aaron deep in his gut. He put his hands on Elisha's shoulders and said with fierce resolve:

"I am *not* goin' anywhere."

Elisha hugged Aaron for the first time. It shocked Aaron, and he wasn't sure what to do with himself. He fought back hard against the tightness in his throat and the stinging in his eyes.

Rav Kadosh waited. He still couldn't bend his fingers, and he had to reach a presentable age before going home to Bruria. He tried to see what time it was, but his vision was so blurry that he couldn't tell if he was wearing his watch. He became increasingly frustrated, and then nasty thoughts started creeping into his mind until he quickly admonished himself. He honestly hated how grumpy he acted every time Elisha came to visit him. It was terrible how old age could do that to a person. He probably shouldn't have been so harsh on the boy. It wasn't like he had done anything *intentionally*. Well, at least he hadn't divulged to Elisha his *whole* score card . . .

A painful stab of arthritis shot up Rav Kadosh's arm, and then another one jolted through his leg. He held back a scream and then a cantankerous mood overwhelmed him. He suddenly felt as bitter as wormwood. *The child was a reckless cataclysm, a walking 9th of Av!* In one summer he had already cut short the life of his great-grandfather by at least ten years . . . Professor Bezalel was as good as dead . . . he had empowered that rogue psychopath student of Professor Bezalel's, and they needed that like a *hole in the head*. And, of course, there was that utter disaster when he was only three years old. *The boy was barely 11!* Lord only knows what they could expect by the time he came of age! Rav Kadosh looked down at his gnarled hands. Even through his hazy vision they were so misshapen that they didn't remotely resemble hands. One thing was clear. There would only be one man left standing—that mutant Kohen . . . who ever heard of a high priest that was one of the 36? But what good was it when the man was a basket case!

Rav Kadosh breathed in deeply and then was surprised to feel his big left toe starting to wiggle. The sensation quickly spread to both his feet and legs. He exhaled with relief and squinted at his hands. *Finally.* They seemed to be close to 80 years old. He opened and closed them with relish. *It was wonderful to feel so young again.* And with it came a surge of renewed optimism. He suddenly felt like he didn't have a care in the world. Why had he gotten so worked up? Everything was coming up roses. The Master of the Universe had entrusted the *greatest* Master Mind who ever lived with His Master Plan. Elisha was adorable when you thought about it . . .

Rav Kadosh knew it was silly, but it was as if his feet and hands had a mind of their own. He started dancing around the room. This *was* the week that would determine the 9th of Av. *The verdict was in!* He did the Hokey Pokey and he turned himself around. *This year was win-all!* Rav Kadosh suddenly stopped his dance in mid-step and, clutching at his chest, dropped to the cold stone floor.

It was the last day of Tammuz, and the royal servant sat upon his throne. This servant had been granted unlimited human wisdom, but that was infinitesimal in comparison to Infinite Wisdom. It did however, make him infinitely wiser than any human being who ever was, is or will be.

He focused on a central spot of his Ispaklaria and then contemplated all the people who concerned him. What he saw was chaos. The last stage of extreme chaos, and it was everywhere. A wide smile brightened his wise face. It was a smile born from the knowledge that chaos was the highest level of the creative process. Chaos contained *all* the potential ingredients they required. Once formation took place, some of that endless potential was always lost along the way. He knew that, unfortunately, those experiencing the chaos would perceive it as horrendous, rather than *perfectly* horrendous.

Today chaos would end, and tomorrow the newly-formed potential would move into action. He was utterly relieved. Relieved that the Master of the Universe had not withheld even the minutest element of chaos . . .

King Solomon then rose from his throne and turned north toward the direction of the Temple and quietly implored: "Now that the time is coming, *please* just hasten it."

He then faced the Ispaklaria and called out: "My dearest sister, my beloved one, let us arise early to the vineyards; let us see whether the vine has blossomed. It is time to unlock the garden and for you to leave your room."

GLOSSARY OF TERMS AND NAMES

An asterisk* indicates a fictional term.

9th of Av (*Tisha B'Av* in Hebrew): An annual fast day which commemorates the destruction of both Temples in Jerusalem, the First Temple by the Babylonians (3338/420 BCE), and the Second Temple by the Romans (3830/70 CE). In Biblical times, it marked the date when the Israelites cried and protested against entering the Promised Land after hearing a bad report from the twelve spies that Moses had sent out to observe the land. They were punished by wandering 40 years in the desert until that entire generation died out. The 9th of Av continued to be a catastrophic date on the Jewish calendar (from the destruction of both Temples to the Spanish Expulsion and even through World War I and World War II). Traditionally, the 9th of Av is also known as a day of potential redemption. Elisha Davidson's birthday is on the 9th of Av.

36: According to Jewish tradition, there are 36 truly selfless people who exist throughout the world at any given time, and it is only on account of these 36 special people that the world doesn't self-destruct. The identity of the 36 is hidden and is not to be revealed. They are often unknown to each other and even to themselves. In Hebrew the 36 are called the *Lamed Vav Tzadikim.*

Ashmodai: The legendary 'King of the Demons,' antagonist and sometime collaborator of King Solomon. There are several legends surrounding the adventures of King Solomon and Ashmodai; in one, Solomon enlists Ashmodai's help in building the Temple.

Av: A Hebrew month that falls in the summertime (July-August). It is the 11th month on the Jewish calendar year. Its first nine days—the "Nine Days"—are days of mourning, culminating in the 9th of Av (*see* above).

Avarshina: A legendary creature in Torah literature similar to the phoenix, who according to Western myth incinerates herself on her nest and is reborn from the ashes. According to the Talmud, Noah found the Avarshina hiding in the hold of the Ark. He said to it, "Do you not want food?" It replied, "I saw that you were busy, and I didn't want to trouble you." He said to it, "May it be His will that you never die, as it is says, 'I shall expire with my nest . . . I shall increase my days.'"

220   ELISHA DAVIDSON AND THE ISPAKLARIA

Azariah: The High Priest during the reign of King Solomon.

Benaiah: King Solomon's chief minister.

*Chamber Seven Graduate: Initiates who have completed all seven levels of North Temple Mount Academy's' Chambers program (*see* Chambers Program), also known as Fifth Dimensional Luminaries (*see* Fifth Dimensional Luminary).

*Chambers Program: The North Temple Mount Academy's clandestine summer school, held in the Foundation Vault (*see* Foundation Vault) in Jerusalem's Old City for grades 6–12, which trains its initiates in an ancient and mystical path of empowerment. The Chambers Program commences every year on the 17th of Tammuz and ends on the last day of Av. Chamber Seven is the highest attainable level. The concept is based on the esoteric *Heichalot* (Chambers) or *Merkavah* (Chariot) literature from the Talmudic period (1st–2nd century CE), which recounts the visions and dangerous mystical journeys of Talmudic sages during their seven-stage ascent into celestial realms. The adepts of this mystical school, also known as *Merkavah* mystics, required elaborate preparation (purification, knowledge of proper incantations, secret Divine names, angelic seals, etc.) in order to navigate the spiritual forces at work in these otherworldly spheres or 'chambers.' The famous Talmudic sage Rabbi Akiva features prominently in the *Heichalot* literature.

Choshen stone: The *Choshen* was the mysterious breastplate which was worn by the High Priest in the Temple in Jerusalem and which served as an oracle. It had twelve different large gems ('*Choshen* stones'), each engraved with the name of one of the tribes of Israel. (In Part One of the Elisha Davidson Trilogy, Elisha discovered a *Choshen* stone from the tribe of Judah on the 17th of Tammuz. The *Choshen* stone activates the Ispaklaria key.)

Eighth Kingdom: According to legend and the mystical book, the Zohar, "God built worlds and destroyed them," before He created the universe as we know it. In Lurianic Kabbalah these worlds are correlated to the eight Edomite Kings in Genesis. Seven of these worlds were destroyed, and we are now in the Eighth Kingdom.

Fifth Dimension: The Kabbalistic *Sefer Yetzirah* (Book of Creation) describes a five-dimensional continuum in which the fifth dimension is the moral-spiritual dimension, also called 'soul.'

GLOSSARY   221

*Fifth Dimensional Luminary: A term used by the North Temple Mount Academy's Chambers Program to describe individuals who have mastered at least the Seventh level of the Chambers Program. It is also used to mean a *Mekubal*, a Kabbalah master (*see* Kabbalah; *see Mekubal*).

Foundation Stone: The 'Foundation Rock' or 'Foundation Stone' (*Even Hashtiyah* in Hebrew), is considered in Judaism to be the holiest spot on earth. It is located on Mount Moriah in Jerusalem, where both the First and Second Temple were erected. Inside the Temples, it was the spot where the Ark of the Covenant stood in the Holy of Holies. According to the Talmud, it is the site where earth was gathered for the creation of Adam, where Cain and Abel and Noah offered sacrifices, where Abraham was tested with the sacrifice of Isaac, and where Jacob had his dream of the ladder. It is also traditionally considered the point where the world was created and a junction of the spiritual and physical universe. (The Dome of the Rock mosque is allegedly constructed on the Foundation Stone.)

*Foundation Vault: A dimensionless void, located in a highly-restricted area underneath the original Temple's foundations on Mount Moriah in Jerusalem, where the North Temple Mount Academy holds its Chambers Program. Chambers initiates can gain access to the Foundation Vault only if they are accompanied by Professor Bezalel or if they're Chamber Seven Graduates. The Foundation Vault is so named because of its close proximity to the 'Foundation Stone' (*see* Foundation Stone).

Ispaklaria: A term used in the Talmud and in mystical texts with various meanings. An Ispaklaria has been described as a clear lens of vision or transcendental reflection, a window hewn from translucent stone, a window of prophecy, a mirror-like reflection of one's heart and soul. In the Elisha Davidson Trilogy the Ispaklaria is defined (by Rav Kadosh in Part One) as "ultimate reality . . . like a tear in the veil, a crack in the wall, a world without its mask, a world with no illusions, and not bound by the 'laws of nature'—no dimensions of space, time or even being."

Kabbalah: A name for Jewish mysticism, whose literal meaning is "receiving."

King Solomon: The third King of Israel and the son of King David and Batsheva. The name 'Solomon,' *Shlomo*, literally means 'peaceful' in Hebrew (he had many other names, including *Kohelet*). King Solomon's 40-

year reign (2917–2957/844–804 BCE) was the golden age of Israel's Kingdom and was characterized by wisdom, riches and splendor. According to rabbinic tradition, Solomon was twelve years old when he ascended the throne and received his Divine gift of wisdom, making him the wisest man to have ever lived. The most important of Solomon's acts was building the Temple—the House of God—on Mount Moriah in Jerusalem, which was one of the wonders of the ancient world. He started construction in the fourth year of his reign (when he was 16 years old) and completed it seven years later. There are many colorful legends recounting the miraculous and magical events that took place during the Temple's construction, including the use of the *Shamir* (*see Shamir*), as well as King Solomon's supernatural powers and dominion over the worlds of demons, angels, and spirits. One of Solomon's contemporaries was the beautiful and brilliant Queen of Sheba, who visited him and was overwhelmed by his wisdom. King Solomon authored three Biblical books: Mishlei (Proverbs), Shir Hashirim (Song of Songs), and Kohelet (Ecclesiastes).

Kohen Gadol: High Priest

Manna: The miraculous food ('bread from heaven,') that nourished the Israelites during their 40-year wanderings in the desert. According to the Torah, the manna descended during the night and was like 'coriander-seed' and 'frost on the ground.' The Israelites would gather it in the morning and cook or bake it. Moses' brother, Aaron, was told to put an omer of manna in a jar as a safekeeping for generations. Leftover manna would rot and turn into maggots. According to legend, the manna took on the flavor of whatever food an individual wanted.

Mekubal: A Kabbalah master (*see* Kabbalah).

Merkavah: Literally 'chariot.' Refers to Ezekiel's extraordinary vision of a heavenly 'chariot' or throne driven by spectacular creatures (Ezekiel Chapter 1). According to many authorities, the imagery of the *Merkavah* is not to be taken literally, and there is great rabbinic opposition to studying this topic as it can be misunderstood. According to legend, King Solomon's throne was fashioned to resemble the *Merkavah*. The early kabbalistic schools were also known as the '*Merkavah* Mystics,' and the study of the *merkavah* was considered secret doctrine entrusted only to the most exemplary and pious scholars. The passage in Ezekiel about the *Merkavah* is read on the holiday of Shavuot, and the *Merkavah* is also referenced in several places in Jewish prayerbooks.

GLOSSARY

Shamir: While there are several legends surrounding the mysterious *Shamir*, no one actually knows what it is or was. It is referred in various places as a creature, being, stone, substance, or special worm. It was endowed with properties that enabled it to cut through stone, iron and precious gems. Thus it was a vital 'tool' in building Solomon's Temple in Jerusalem since the use of iron tools was prohibited (objects of war and bloodshed were deemed inappropriate to be used in building the Temple which promoted peace). According to legend, Moses used the *Shamir* to engrave the *Choshen* stones (see *Choshen*). Legend relates that King Solomon searched everywhere for the *Shamir* and discovered its location though Ashmodai, the King of the Demons. King Solomon captured the Shamir and used its special powers to build the First Temple. The *Shamir* was wrapped in wool and stored in a container made of lead, because any other substance would disintegrate under the *Shamir's* gaze. The *Shamir* was said either to have been lost or to have lost its potency after the First Temple was destroyed.

Shekel: The State of Israel's currency.

Tammuz: A Hebrew month that falls in the summertime (June-July). It is the tenth month on the Jewish calendar year. The 17th of Tammuz is a fast day that marks the breaching of Jerusalem's walls by the Babylonians and later by the Romans, which led to the destruction of both Temples on the 9th of Av (*see* 9th of Av). It is the beginning of the 'Three Weeks', which is a countdown to the 9th of Av. During this period joyous occasions are restricted.

Tahash: An animal mentioned in the Torah and in the Talmud. Its skin was used to beautify the *Mishkan* (Tabernacle). According to various legends, the Tahash was a unicorn with beautiful multi-colored skin (blue and violet in color or like a rainbow). The Tahash only existed temporarily when the Israelites built the *Mishkan* in the desert, and then it disappeared.

Tehillim: Psalms

Yessod: Literally 'foundation.' *Yessod* is one of the ten *Sephirot* (attributes or emanations of the Infinite One in Kabbalah). It is associated in the soul with the power to contact, connect and communicate with outer reality. In this trilogy Elisha Davidson is called the *Yessod*—the *One Who Connects.*

ELISHA DAVIDSON
and the Ispaklaria
(Part Two of a Trilogy)

*The following is a partial list of sources that have been used
in the writing of the Elisha Davidson Trilogy.*

1. **Torah with Rashi commentary:**
   Shemot (Exodus), *Vayikra* (Leviticus), *Bamidbar* (Numbers).

2. ***Nevi'im* (Prophets) with Rashi commentary:**
   Melachim I & II (Kings I & II), *Yirmeyahu* (Jeremiah), *Yechezkel*
   (Ezekiel).

3. ***Ketuvim* (Writings) with Rashi commentary:**
   Shir Hashirim (The Song of Songs), *Eicha* (Lamentations), *Kohelet*
   (Ecclesiastes), *Divrei Hayamim* (Chronicles).

4. **Talmud Bavli — Ein Yaakov (Legends of the Babylonian Talmud):**
   *Brachot, Shabbat, Pessachim, Yoma, Ta'anit, Megillah, Chagigah,
   Sotah, Gittin, Kiddushin, Bava Batra, Sanhedrin, Avodah Zarah,
   Menachot, Chullin.*

5. ***Midrash Rabbah***

6. ***Mishkney Elyon*** (Secrets of the Future Temple),
   Rabbi Moshe Chaim Luzzatto, translated by Rabbi Avraham
   Greenbaum, 1999.

7. **The Western Wall Tunnels: Touching the Stones of our Heritage**,
   Dan Bahat, 2002.

8. **Carta's Illustrated Encyclopedia of The Holy Temple in Jerusalem**,
   Israel Ariel and Chaim Richman, 2005.

9. **Sefer Yetzirah (The Book of Creation: In Theory and Practice)**,
   translation and commentary by Rabbi Aryeh Kaplan, 1997.

10. **Meditation and the Kabbalah**, Rabbi Aryeh Kaplan, 1985.

11. **Meditation and the Bible**, Rabbi Aryeh Kaplan, 1988.

12. **Jewish Meditation: A Practical Guide**, Rabbi Aryeh Kaplan, 1995.

13. **Seeing God**, Rabbi David Aaron, 2001.

14. **Mysterious Creatures**, Nosson Slifkin, 2003.

Author's Biography

Rhonda Attar (nee Antelman) was born and educated in the U.S. (M.S. TV/Radio) and made Aliyah to Israel where she became a leading figure in the Israeli television industry launching 10 TV channels—6 in Israel and 4 worldwide. Mrs. Attar and her husband Rabbi Meir Attar are the co-founders and directors of the Tomer Devorah Beit Knesset, 24/7 Beit Midrash, and Kolel Chatzot in Kochav Ya'akov dedicated to *V'ahavta L'rayeicha Kamocha* (Love your Neighbor like yourself).

*Soon to be released in the
Elisha Davidson Trilogy:*

ELISHA DAVIDSON
and the Shamir